The Word Became Verse

A Paraverse of John's Gospel

Lee Venden

Illustrated by
Dalene Johnson

Published by All About Jesus Seminars
www.allaboutjesusseminars.org

This book was
Edited by Lorene Ford
Cover and interior designed by Tim Larson
Cover art and Illustrations by Dalene Johnson
Typeset: Cantoria MT 12/14

Printed in Canada

ISBN 978-0-578-33313-7

Prologue

Recently my mother, Marilyn, who is a hospice patient, expressed her desire that her heart might be more deeply stirred by the Gospels. Like many Christians who have worn out their Bibles, she'd become so familiar with the stories they didn't seem as fresh. Familiarity can sometimes desensitize and she longed for an Emmaus Road experience with Jesus that caused her heart to "burn within her."

I recalled some forty-five years earlier weeping over the death of Aslan in Lewis's "Chronicles of Narnia." As my eyes spilled over, I wondered why the same emotion didn't overtake me while reading in the Bible about the Crucifixion of Jesus. *Why am I not as deeply touched by that?* I thought.

At that moment, on my bed in my basement room, the Spirit whispered into my consciousness, "But you *ARE* touched by the death of Jesus! That's why the death of Aslan has such an impact on you. You just needed to hear the old, old story in a fresh way to discover it has lost none of its impact."

In the decades that have followed, I have collected dozens and dozens of books on the life of Jesus: Oursler, Lewis, Rasmussen, Keller, White, Miller, Hardinge, Spurgeon, Lucado, Thielicke, Manning, Venden, Bishop, Holmes, Card, Lloyd, Richards, Marciano, Yancy, Johnson, Gire, and Gregory, to name a few. Not to mention numerous paraphrases and translations of the Bible. Each book in its turn gives me a fresh perspective on the greatest story ever told. I know I will never tire of that Story, since every re-telling strikes an answering chord in my heart. The best Christian music and poetry does the same thing to me.

In response to my mother's expressed desire, I brought her several books from those I've collected, only to find she'd read each of them numerous times before. Then an almost forgotten dream of mine re-visited me. It had come and gone sporadically over the years. *Why not write your favorite Gospel as poetry?*

The task seemed overwhelmingly impossible. Each time the idea had knocked, I had retreated into a back room and left the door unanswered. But my Mom is dying now, and she has this last wish to have her heart stirred one more time with gratitude, love, and appreciation for the One towards whom she is hastening.

What would happen, I thought, *if I at least gave it a try? Maybe I'd be surprised by the results? Maybe the idea has been inspired by Someone bigger than me? Maybe the One who is The Word could pour thoughts with rhythm and rhyme through my aging brain?*

So having said a prayer (and subsequently many more), I sat down and was astounded by what materialized on the screen of my iPad. I'm convinced it was a gift! Like all the other authors I mentioned, it was given so that in the re-telling of the old, old story, we, and those who read what we write, would find the fire in our hearts once again blazing and bringing warmth.

This "para-verse" is not offered as a literal translation or deep theological treatise. Rather, it is my hope that the reading will bounce nimbly from page to page, carrying the reader eagerly along -maybe even becoming difficult to put down.

As I have worked through each chapter and verse, I have read and re-read the passages in a variety of different Bible translations. In so doing, I've discovered that some translations include or omit things other translations don't include or omit. These verses I have written are a synthesis, or partial "harmony of the translations" I have read.

I will also confess that at times the muse overtook me and I wove a thought or two of my own into the narrative. I ask the reader to be gracious unto me for this, and to not lay this "sin" to my charge.

During the month that this book was being birthed, I read several draft chapters to my fading Mother for her consideration. Each time I did, a light came into her eyes, a smile crossed her tired face, she sat just a little more erect in her hospital bed and she gave me a semi-vigorous thumbs-up. "I hope you finish it before I die!" she would say. "It's doing the job!"

Lee Venden, January 3, 2020

Acknowledgments

I wish to credit and thank the Spirit of God for giving me words, rhyme, and an enthusiasm for this project that exponentially exceeds any natural abilities of my own. In short, this project has been a gift from start to finish.

I wish to express gratitude to Dalene Johnson for her passion for John's Gospel and Lord, for meditating on the life of Christ with a brush in her hand, for countless wee hours transforming words into watercolors, and for sharing the results with me.

Many thanks to Lorene Ford, a wordsmith and mentor who prayerfully read through my drafts offering suggestions and tweaks that took a good thing and made it better. She truly caught the Spirit of this project and partnered with me endlessly to transform it into black and white.

I am also grateful for another disciple whom Jesus loves, Marji Venden, my wife, partner and friend for 43 years. Her prayers for me and this project and her willingness to listen to draft after draft were a great encouragement. She is a disciple loved by Lee as well.

Descending Into Greatness

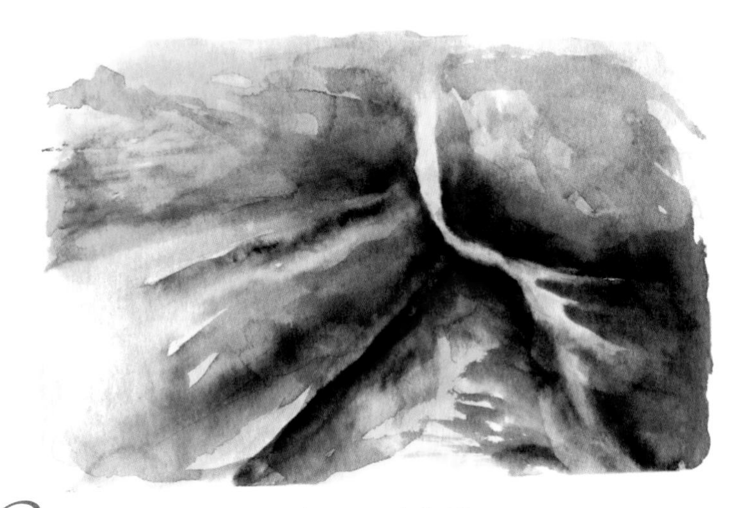

Chapter 1:1-18

Long before the world began the Word already was.
In fact, our earth was born of Him —He is the Primal Cause.
And like the sun He is the Light for souls in darkness bound;
A blaze that dark cannot withstand or hold its feeble ground.

God sent a man whose name was John to baptize and declare
That Jesus came to be the Light for people everywhere.
But though He was Creator God, of earth and all contained,
He was by most unrecognized, rejected and profaned.

Yet some there were who followed Him, of women and of men.
To them He gave the right to be God's children —born again.
Because the Word became a man and lived with us awhile,
It's possible for us to leave these heartaches, tears and trials.

John testified, "He is the One! The Father's only Son!
He lived and reigned the universe before time had begun."
And from His fullness we receive rich grace beyond compare;
Blessings, favors, gifts and more —so *much* that we can share.

The decalogue through Moses given left more to be desired.
But God's great love through Jesus Christ has in our hearts inspired
A vision of the joy and hope that takes away all fear.
We see instead His faithfulness -Christ Jesus brought Him near.

Chapter 1:19-34

The leaders questioned, was this John the long awaited One?
Yet he denied, and then affirmed the promised time *had* come.
"My job is to prepare the way, a pathway for the Lord,
For He is coming to proclaim what's written in God's Word."

"The One Who's coming after me surpasses me by far,
For He existed long before His birth announced by stars.
And I have not, as yet, beheld the glory of His face.
I am unworthy to untie His sandal's leather lace."

The next day Jesus came to John in Jordan's watery wave,
Insisting that John baptize Him for He was there to save.
Beneath the water He was laid, this One who knew no sin,
And John's strong voice was heard that day in testament of Him.

"I saw the Spirit like a dove, in glorious rays descend.
In dazzling splendor it came down and hovered over Him.
'You'll know,' God said, 'by what you see, that He's my chosen One.'
So now I say with certainty, He *is* God's only Son!"

Chapter 1: 35-51

Next day John spoke, as Jesus passed, "There goes the Lamb of God."
Two of his disciples heard and thought that title odd.
So they set off to follow Christ and tagged along behind.
But Jesus turned and kindly asked, "What do you hope to find?"

Then one of them said, "Rabbi please, where is it that You stay?
If You don't mind we'd like to come and hear all that You say."
"I do not mind," He answered them. "You're welcome --come and see.
In fact, I'm very pleased you want to spend the day with Me."

The two of them, Andrew and John, delighted and inspired,
Stayed with Christ till day was done without becoming tired.
Then Andrew went excitedly to share with yet another.
"We've found Messiah," he exclaimed to Simon, his own brother.

Simon came to Jesus next, left nets, and boats, and water.
Jesus, looking at him said, "Your name shall now be Peter."
Next day they went to Galilee where Philip had his home.
The Savior said, "Come follow Me --don't stay here all alone."

But just before accepting this invitation grand,
Philip thought of his good friend and hurriedly he ran
To find Nathanael where he sat, absorbed in thought and prayer.
Cried Philip, "We have found Him sought by people everywhere!"

"He is the One whom Moses wrote would set all Israel free.
He hails from Nazareth. If you'll come, I'm certain you will see."
"Can any good come from that place?" Nathanael mocked and frowned.
"Come see," said Philip, "we must go before He leaves our town."

Nathanael yielded to the pleas, and couldn't hide surprise
That Jesus complimented him while looking in his eyes.
When Jesus said, "I saw you there," Nathanael was awed,
And bowing low he worshiped Him. "You *are* the Son of God!"

"You are the King of Israel, the heir to David's throne.
You are worthy to be praised and worshiped. You alone!"
Jesus answered, "Greater things are certain to astound!
You will see the heavens split and angels coming down!"

Chapter 2:1-12

In the tiny town of Cana, which is part of Galilee,
A wedding party ate and drank in festive jubilee.
Christ's mother worked the kitchen in her task to oversee
The direction of the servants as she helped whole-heartedly.

Christ had been invited too along with all His men,
And many at the wedding feast were whispering of them.
It seems the Baptist had proclaimed He was God's only Son,
And all were wondering what that meant. *Had the Messiah come?*

Provisions started running low and so Christ's mother said,
"My Son, the wine's completely gone although we still have bread."
Jesus' answer puzzled her, "My time has not yet come."
"What does He mean?" she asked herself, yet trusted in her Son.

And so, while pondering His response, she called some servants who
Were standing near and said to them, "Whatever He says, do!"
Six granite jars were close at hand —each large enough we're told
That every one, when filled to brim, could thirty gallons hold.

"Please fill those jars," the Savior said, "with water, cool and pure.
Then dip a cup and take it to that man just over there
Who is the Master of the Feast. And once he's sampled some
You'll find there's wine enough to serve each wedding guest who's come."

The Master of the feast could not believe what he'd been given!
"This wine," he said, "it tastes so good, it must have come from Heaven!"

Each wedding guest agreed with him and asked the servants how
It happened that they'd "saved the best and only served it now."

"Miraculous!" the servants said and when they'd shared their story,
It seemed to each and everyone that they had seen Christ's glory.
The Lord's disciples who were there believed from that day on,
And possibly His mother mused, "Perhaps His time *has* come!"

Chapter 2:13-25

Passover time was drawing near and Jews from every land
Were journeying to Jerusalem, all traveling in bands.
With His disciples Jesus came to worship and to praise,
But at the temple He stopped short. Confusion met His gaze.

He saw the merchants selling there with cattle, lambs and doves.
He saw them make a racket of His Father's gift of love.
He saw exchangers' tables where the people cursed and swore.
He saw their ever-reaching hands and heard demands of "More!"

He stiffened as He made a whip from strands of rope He found.
He raised His arm and suddenly one couldn't hear a sound.
His eyes flashed fire as He drove the livestock out the door,
And the clang of money-changer's coins went rattling 'cross the floor.

"Take these things out," He cried with pain that could not be disguised.
"You've turned my Father's house into a place of merchandise.
Grace can't be bought, it's not for sale, and money has no weight.
It's meant to be a *Gift*, you see, let's set the record straight."

Then it was His followers remembered Scripture's phrase.
They saw how Jesus cared about perceptions in that place.
"He has such passion for God's house," they said to one another,
But the leaders frowned and stewed, made angry by the bother.

"What right have You," those leaders cried, "to do what You have done?
To call this place Your Father's house as if You are His Son!
You're just a man like all of us – Your worth You overrate.
You're nothing but a commoner imagining You're great."

"All right," said Jesus, "I'll give you a sign you can't deny.
Destroy this temple and in three days I'll raise it to the sky."
"Now You've gone mad!" they screamed in rage. "Five decades in the making.
The construction of this place was no small undertaking."

"Three days? You fool! Do you presume one man could have such power?"
Their rage, like brimstone, made their words a scattering angry shower.
"You have heard," Christ answered them, "but haven't understood.
Perhaps it's far too much to think that any of you would."

The temple He referred to was His body, scourged and torn.
The three-day rebuild would be seen on resurrection morn.
That Sunday, three years later, when His tomb burst open wide,
His followers remembered what before He'd prophesied.

The fickle crowd who witnessed this encounter Jesus had
Determined they would follow Him —which left the leaders mad.
But Jesus wasn't fooled by this. He knew right from the start,
Like wind-blown reeds they'd bend and sway. He knew each person's heart.

Chapter 3:1-21

Nicodemus was a man, a leader of the Jews,
Who was renowned throughout the land and honored for his views.
A member of the Sanhedrin, well recognized by all,
A teacher come by night to see the Lord outside the wall.

He came by night so he could hide from prying eyes in town.
"Good Rabbi, You must be from God. Your miracles abound!"

"I'd like to talk, if You don't mind, about the things of Heaven.
I'm guessing You could shed some light for You've been wisdom given."

More rapidly than one might think, the Master made reply,
"You do not understand as yet. You look through darkened eyes.
I tell you this, and it is true, unless you're born again,
You'll never see the things of God but just the things of men."

"What do you mean," this leader said. "How can a man return
Into his mother's womb? It seems impossible to learn."
"Impossible with *man*," said Christ, "for pauper or for king.
It must be supernatural. It is a Spirit thing."

"It takes the Spirit to bring forth the supernatural life.
It never will result from just a husband and a wife.
The wind blows as it wills and you can never tell from where.
But you can see the leaves astir —like on that tree right there."

"It's like that with the Spirit, which you can't control at all.
He moves where *He* determines to and not by beck and call.
But when He stirs inside your heart, His presence you can tell.
It changes all you say and do and what you think as well."

"How *can* these things be possible Lord?" Nicodemus asked.
"I want this change You talk about. I'm burdened with that task."

"If truth were known I've felt the need, though teacher I may be,
For something more than surface life. I really want to *see*!"

"All right," said Christ, "I know your heart and that you are sincere.
There is one thing that you can do to bring the Spirit near.
As Moses lifted the bronze snake amid the desert sands,
The Son of God must be raised up and gazed upon by man."

"I promise if you look My way and breathe a heartfelt prayer,
It matters not how strong your faith; My Spirit will be there.
Your heart will stir, your soul rejoice, and you will know, My friend,
The Holy Spirit's done His work and you've been born again."

"For this is why My Father sent His well-beloved Son,
That everyone who trusts in Him, no matter what they've done,
Need never perish but can live in bliss forevermore.
The serpent in the desert actually represents the Door."

"And judgment doesn't fall on those who trust the Father's Son.
But those who do not trust in Him are totally undone.
You must understand," said Christ, "that trust is based on knowing
Someone who is dependable —in whom your faith is growing."

"You've come to see Me in the dark but for you Light's been blazing.
The fact so many love the night's both troubling and amazing.
Sadly, they detest what's bright and stay away in fear,
But those reborn cling to the Light --enjoying being near!"

Chapter 3:22-36

John's disciples held a grudge, resenting Jesus' words.
They thought John was slighted and were jealous of the Lord.
They voiced their deep concern to John that crowds were getting thin.
"Everyone is following Christ. He draws all men to Him."

John said, "No man has a thing that isn't from Above.
We *all* heard the Father's voice and saw the Heavenly Dove.
You know I'm not Messiah. I was sent to go before,
To simply help make straight the way and open up the door."

"We know that at a wedding it's the *Groom* who gets the bride,
So I am filled with joyfulness to come along beside.
He must become greater. He's the One who's above all.
I must become less and less. Beside *Him* I am small."

"I am of the earth, you know, and speak of earthly things.
But Jesus comes from Heaven where majestic angels sing.
There's no one that's above Him. He is greater and by *far*!
But He calls us to come to Him in spite of who we are."

"What's sad is that so few believe the things He has to say.
They don't perceive He speaks God's words and points us Heaven's way.
God's given Him the Spirit *full* and placed *all* in His hand!
If only more would grasp these things and truly understand!"

"For anyone who trusts in Him, believing He's God's Son,
Will live forevermore one day when this life's journey's done.
But those who don't receive Him now and won't believe His Word
Will someday fall in judgment at the coming of the Lord."

Chapter 4:1-42

In part to ease the tension that John's disciples felt,
Jesus went to Samaria and there for two days dwelt.
He paused just outside Sychar to rest near Jacob's well
While His disciples went to town, where merchants buy and sell.

To satisfy their hunger, they hoped to buy some bread.
"I'll wait right here beside the well," their weary Master said.
Close to noon a woman came, with pitcher, there to draw,
And as she tied the rope secure, a Stranger there she saw.

He'd been intently watching her and now made a request
Which startled her! He was a Jew—she knew by how He dressed.
"If it isn't too much trouble, could you share a drink with Me?
This heat has made Me thirsty. Water would so welcome be!"

She couldn't believe He was speaking to her.
That was something a Jew wouldn't do!
"How is it You've asked *me* a favor?" she said,
"I wouldn't expect that from You."

Jesus replied to her, "Woman,
If you knew the Gift of God,
And Who is asking for a drink,
I'm sure you would be awed."

"In fact," He said, "you'd ask *Me* for a drink
And I'd give you living water.
It's better by far than what you draw
From this well, My precious daughter."

The woman replied, "You don't have a rope
So how could You ever draw
This Living water, of which You speak?
Your offer contains a flaw."

"Are You greater than Jacob who dug this well?
And watered his livestock here?
Your conversation amuses me.
You're suffering from sun-stroke I fear."

"Those who drink *this* water," said Christ,
"Will only thirst again.
But the water of which I spoke just now,
Can satisfy without end."

"It's the Water of Life I am talking about
And it wells from 'way deep within.
If you drink it you'll live forever, with joy,
In a world that is free from sin."

"Sir, give me a drink of *that* water," she said,
"I'd love to stop walking out here.
I come from the town to draw from this well.
I'd prefer to have something that's near."

"Go get your husband," said Jesus,
"I'll wait for you both to come back."
"You've asked the impossible," she replied,
"A husband is something I lack."

"You are right about that," answered Jesus,
"For you have been married, times five.
And the man that you're living with now
Hardly knows that you're even alive."

The woman said, "Sir, You're a prophet!
It's really not that hard to see.
I'd like to change the subject and
Discuss something other than me."

"So how about this? My ancestors taught
That we could worship right here.
You Jews say it must be Jerusalem,
Which sadly is not very near."

"The time's coming soon," replied Jesus,
"When worshipers everywhere
Will worship the Father in spirit and truth,
Unconcerned whether here or there."

"Most people have yet to understand that
The Father wants *more* than our minds.
He wants our hearts engaged as well
And all who will seek Him will find."

"He's looking for relationship.
It's not *servants* He wants, it is *friends*.
That's what I meant by 'spirit and truth.'
Is it starting to make any sense?"

The woman replied, "That's too *good* to be true!
If only Messiah were here!
He'd tells us all what to say and to do.
He'd make it abundantly clear!"

Said Jesus, "He who's here talking with you
Is the One you are wishing would come.
I know what I've told you is true because
The Messiah and I are one."

Just then His disciples returned with the food
And couldn't believe their eyes.
That Jesus would speak with a woman like *her*
Filled them with great surprise.

Yet they didn't dare question Him about her,
But stood watching from afar,
As the woman took off in a hurry towards town
—Completely forgetting her jar.

"Come see a man!" she proclaimed as she ran,
"Who just told me all things that I've done!
Could it finally be it's fulfilled prophecy
And this very Man is the One?"

Meanwhile His friends with the food came to Him,
Saying, "Master You really must eat."
But He turned and said, "I've already been fed.
I've had food —though it wasn't meat."

His friends were confused and they said to each other,
"Has someone else given Him food?"
"When working for Heaven, the things one is given,"
Said Christ, "are exceedingly good!"

"Some would say that the time of the harvest's not near.
'Four more months till we gather it in.'
But look at that town and the crowd gathered 'round.
Don't forget we are fishers of *men*."

"Some sow and some reap. That's the way it is done.
But the fruit is a life that's eternal.
And one day when harvesting fields that *I've* sown,
Just remember that mankind's the kernel."

The Samaritan people of Sychar
Hurried out to the well to request
That Jesus would linger there in their town,
For His words gave their hearts peace and rest.

And they wanted to ask Him more questions
While they sat at His feet to learn
About this God who is friendly and
Who wants wayward men to return.

So for two days He stayed with those people
And He spoke to them wonderful things.
Their thirst was quenched like the woman's
And they *too* believed He was King.

"At first we were drawn by *your* words," they told her,
"Inspired by the tone of *your* voice.
But now we've heard Him ourselves and with you,
We also have cause to rejoice."

"He's not just a man, He's the Savior of all
And He's come to rescue our earth.
He is the Christ we've been waiting for.
No treasure compares with His worth!"

Chapter 4:43-54

Now after He'd stayed *there* for two days
Jesus headed for Galilee.
The folks in Nazareth made it clear
His divinity they could not see.

Since a prophet has no honor in
The land that He calls His home,
He continued to travel to places where
He was already known.

Galilee made Him welcome, however,
For they thought His miracles fine!
They remembered the wedding in Cana, where
He'd turned the water to wine.

Nearby, in the town of Capernaum,
There lived an official who had
A son who was sick and dying
—His whole family was grieving and sad!

His heart took hope when he heard the news
That to *their* town Christ had come,
And he rushed to Him where he weeping begged,
"Won't You please come and heal my son?"

Jesus knew that his heart wasn't true,
"Unless you see signs..." He replied.
But the father in desperation pled,
"Please come before he has died!"

Jesus' heart was touched, for He loved him much,
And He said, "You can go your way.
Your son is well and he will grow
To have children himself, someday."

The man believed so he left relieved
And as he was nearing town,
His servants ran out to meet him,
Eagerly gathering 'round.

"He is well!" they cried with excitement.
"The Master has wonderful power!"
"When did he start to get better,"
The father asked them. "What hour?"

"Yesterday afternoon," they replied,
"His fever broke around one."
"That is *exactly* the time," said the man,
"When Jesus said it was done!"

So the nobleman and all his family
Believed in Christ evermore.
Their hearts were no longer troubled by
The doubts they'd had before.

"He's the *Lord* and He's our Savior!"
They shouted both far and near.
And their hearts were so full of gratitude,
It flowed from their eyes as tears.

Compassion And Provision

Chapter 5:1-16

Once while in Jerusalem, not far from the old Sheep Gate,
Beside Bethesda's pool where crowds of people came to wait,
Christ walked alone through colonnades and covered porches five.
Many lay there blind, lame, sick —some barely alive.

There was a legend folks believed, that sometimes angels came
To stir the pool. Those first to plunge would never be the same.
So crowds of the sick and dying, each hoping to be first,
Pushed and shoved, close by the edge, becoming worse and worse.

And there a paralytic lay —a friendless man, alone.
For eight and thirty years or so the pool had been his home.
And Jesus, as He moved among those waiting so forlorn,
Saw this man and suddenly discovered *His* heart torn.

He longed to heal them all that day but knew it could not be.
'Twas Sabbath and the leaders watched, saying, "Just you wait and see!
If He approaches anyone a miracle to perform,
We can apprehend Him then for going against our norms."

So Jesus stood there looking down into the sick man's eyes,
And said to him, "Would you be well? No longer paralyzed?"
The man replied, "There's not a chance. I have no friends, you see.
I'll never be the first to plunge. There is no hope for me."

But Jesus said, "No more of this. That's not the way to talk.
I'm here, so rise up, take your bed, for you shall surely walk."
As strength surged through his feeble limbs, the man *knew* he was well.
Some leaders squinted narrowly and hurried off to tell.

While others of them gathered 'round the healed man and said,
"You're violating Sabbath since you're carrying your bed."
He answered, "He who made me well, said, 'Take your bed and walk.'
I really mustn't linger here or further with you talk."

The leaders angrily began interrogating him.
"Who is it that has healed you and commanded you to sin?"
But Jesus had withdrawn Himself into the crowd, and so,
The man could not respond to them because he did not know.

Then later, Jesus found him in the temple, where He said,
"I'm the One who made you well and told you, 'Take your bed.'
But sin no more, for sin it was that caused you so much pain.
Worse things will surely follow you, if you do *not* refrain."

"Since sin is separation from the Source of Life, you see,
It follows that you'd start to die when separate from Me.
So if you listen to My words and follow them as well,
As years continue passing by you'll enjoy good health still."

The man who had been paralyzed reported to the Jews
That Jesus was the One who'd healed. They rankled at the news.
And they determined then and there that Jesus they would kill.
This Sabbath-breaking rebel they would nail on Calvary's hill.

Chapter 5:17-30

Jesus knew their plotting and He boldly spoke these words,
"My Father works on Sabbath. I'm surprised you haven't heard.
Every heart that's beating is sustained because of Him.
And healing folks on Sabbath certainly is not a sin!"

This provoked the leaders and they sought the more to kill.
"He not only broke the Sabbath, He believes He's God as well."

"I assure you," answered Jesus, "of Myself, I nothing do.
I just focus on my Father and His works come streaming through."

"You're concerned because I healed and told a man to lift his bed?
You'll see more than this for certain! You will see Me raise the dead!
And one thing more, the Father never judges anyone,
Because *that* job's been given to His one and only Son."

"It's His will that all should honor and respect the Son, because
Those who *don't* insult the Father, Who's the *Source* of all He does.
Most assuredly I tell you, those who hear Me and believe
In the Father Who has sent Me, everlasting life receive."

"And they don't come up for judgment but have passed from death to life.
They are saved from this world's toils, heartaches, cares and endless strife.
The time's coming soon, I promise, when the dead Christ's voice shall hear.
Some will shake the grave's cold shackles as He wipes away each tear."

"*That* will only be a foretaste of what's coming down the line.
All the dead will hear that voice when comes the end of time.
Some will rise to life eternal, peace and joy beyond compare.
Others rise to condemnation; in those *joys* they'll have no share."

Chapter 5:31-47

"I'm not asking you to simply take My word, and Mine alone.
There's another who has told you that the Son of Man has come.
John bore witness strongly to Me, though you heard and disbelieved.
Now I've come to share the Good News which would save you if received."

"He was like an oil lamp burning —shining in the dark of night.
For a brief time you were willing to rejoice within his light.
But I have a greater witness than the Baptist's, which was true,
More than words, though rightly spoken, it's the mighty *works* I do."

"Not to mention that the Father testified with shining Dove.
And with *words* that rang like thunder, spoken from the sky above.
Sadly though, you didn't hear Him —for to Him your ears are closed.
Which explains why you won't listen to the One that Heaven chose."

"You have memorized the Scriptures —analyzed from A to Z.
But because your *heart's* not in it, you don't see they point to Me.
I don't seek for your approval since you're empty of God's love.
What you say just doesn't matter, since it isn't from above."

"Though I come endorsed by Heaven, it means not a thing to you.
But the ones who live for *this* world, you approve and follow too.
For you gladly praise each other. You are so impressed by men.
Why do you not care what God thinks? Don't you want to honor Him?"

"Moses will condemn you on the final judgment day.
He who wrote the books you've read will speak up and he'll say,
'Why did you, in spite of reading, fail to trust the Father's Son?
He's the Lamb, the Cloud, the High Priest. He's the Rock. He *is* The One.'"

"Since you listened not to Moses, since you choose to not believe,
There's no way I can persuade you. Gifts I have, you won't receive."

Chapter 6:1-15

Now after this the Savior crossed the Sea of Galilee
And huge crowds formed because they hoped more miracles to see.
Then Christ, with His disciples, climbed a grassy hillside there.
The gathering grew by thousands. There were people everywhere!

As Jesus looked across the crowd and saw the sea of heads,
He turned and questioned Philip, asking, "Where can we buy bread?"
The question wasn't needed since Christ knew what He would do.
He was merely testing Philip, hoping faith would glimmer through.

"There's no way," protested Philip. "We could work for half a year,
But *our* wages couldn't nearly feed the people gathered here."
Then Andrew hesitantly said, "There is a young lad who
Has five small loaves and two small fish —but what could that bit do?"

"Tell everyone to sit down on the grassy slopes," Christ said,
"And bring the boy with those small fish and barley loaves of bread."
Then Jesus, asking God to place His blessing on the meal,
Distributed the food until each person had their fill.

He did this with both loaves and fish, and twenty thousand said
They could *not* have eaten better had they been at home instead.
Then Christ told His disciples, "Gather up what's left right now."
So they filled twelve baskets with the scraps but could not fathom how.

"This is the prophet," said the crowd, "Whom we've been looking for.
Let's make Him king and we'll not suffer Romans anymore."
But Jesus had a different plan than they did on that day.
Amidst their boisterous clamoring, He quietly slipped away.

Chapter 6:16-21

The disciples stayed by waiting near their boat upon the shore,
Where they thought they'd transport Jesus, using sails or just their oars.
But the Lord did not return to them so, as the darkness fell,
They launched out for Capernaum —not feeling very well.

Soon a gale swept down the slopes from mountains near the shore.
Like cork their wind-blown vessel tossed as they pulled on the oars.
They struggled till their muscles cramped and strength they had no more,
While Jesus watched them quietly from on the distant shore.

The sea spoke boisterously of death. The waves kept sweeping 'cross
The bow and stern of their small craft till they cried out, "We're lost!"
'Twas then that suddenly they saw Christ walking on the waves.
He hadn't once forgotten them and now He came to save.

"Is it You?" they shouted loudly calling out to Him in fear.
"Yes it is!" the Lord responded. "All is well for *I Am* here!"
They had paddled several miles. As for progress, there was none.
But once *Christ* stepped aboard that boat their traveling was done!

Just like that, the storm had stopped and they were still alive.
Their craft and all its cargo at Capernaum arrived!
They'd been sure that all was lost; been frightened to the core.
Then instantly, with Jesus, they were at the other shore.

Chapter 6:22-40

The following day, across the lake, the folks who had been fed
Came back to look for Jesus –they were hoping for more bread.
But after searching high and low they found no trace of Him,
So booking passage they set off for old Capernaum.

They crossed the lake and were amazed to find that He was *there*!
In disbelief they said, "Rabbi, we searched 'most everywhere!
Please tell us how it is that You came clear across the sea?"
Said Jesus sadly in reply, "You do not care for Me."

"You're just seeking, hoping for more blessings, gifts and things.
I'd prefer you were concerned for all salvation brings.
Don't just labor for the food that perishes for sure.
Seek instead the Living Bread --the food that will endure."

"For everlasting life is what I came to offer most,
And not to simply cater meals or be a gracious host.
For God the Father sent His Son to offer you much more!
And if you will accept Him, He will be for you the Door."

"You speak of God," the people said. "What is it He requires?
Tell us plainly what He wants —what is it He desires?"
"This is what God wants," Christ said, "that you'd believe in Me,
And trust the One He sent so you can live eternally."

"What sign will You perform," they asked, "to prove that You're the One?
He gave our fathers manna as they wandered 'neath the sun."

"You believe that Moses was the giver of that bread,
But God the Father was the One who gave it," Jesus said.

"He still desires to give to you the true Bread sent from Heaven.
I Am the Manna He has sent —the Son whom He has given.
The Bread of God is He who comes from Heaven down to earth
To give His life that you might live and find eternal worth."

"Sir," they said, "give us that bread and we'll be satisfied."
"I'm telling you, I *Am* the Bread of Life," the Lord replied.
"Whoever comes to Me will find he hungers nevermore.
And those who trust Me cease to thirst for things —and that is sure."

"I've told you this, and you have heard, but *still* you don't believe.
Yet those the Father sends to Me, I gladly will receive.
For I came down from Heaven not to do My will, you see.
I came to do the will of God —the Father who sent Me."

"And more than anything He wants to see each person saved,
That I not lose a single one of those to Me He gave.
He wants each one to trust the Son, to look to Him and live.
Then I will raise them up one day, eternal life to give."

Chapter 6:41-59

At this the Jews began to grouse, "What is this that He said?
He thinks that He is from above and that He's 'Living Bread?'
This is absurd and cannot be! We know where He came from!
He's just a man from Nazareth. He's only Joseph's son."

"Stop grumbling among yourselves," said Jesus in reply.
"No one ever understands the wherefores, hows or whys
Unless My Father gives to them a supernatural eye.
But those who grasp the things I say, I'll raise up by and by."

"Those who *heed* the voice of God and love the things He's taught
Will see in Me, the Father's Son, the *Answers* they have sought.
And if you listen to My words I'll tell you what *He's* like.
And furthermore, I'll give to you an everlasting life."

"The manna that you spoke about did not sustain your fathers.
They all died and in that place were buried with the others.
But I'm the Bread of Life, the One descended from the sky,
And all who eat the Bread that's Me will live and never die."

"This 'Bread' I am referring to? It is My flesh and blood.
I'm giving it without reserve. I'm here to save this world."
The Jews responded angrily, "He thinks that we could eat
His flesh and blood for food? How strange! His body like it's *meat*?"

"It is a fact," replied the Lord, "the words I've said are true!
If you refuse to eat My flesh, you have no life in you.
But all who eat My flesh and blood in this world filled with strife,
Will live forevermore with Me –they'll have eternal life."

"You see, life's not just physical, it's spiritual as well.
These symbols I have spoken of have deeper meaning still.
What I am trying to explain is how to live and grow,
And how to live life *spiritually* is what you need to know."

"I draw life from up above, depending on My Father.
And He's the One who feeds *My* soul with Heavenly bread and water.
So it is with you and Me, if you will eat *this* Bread,
I will sustain your soul and be your *spirit's* life," Christ said.

"To be clear, I will repeat and say it one more time.
The manna your ancestors ate? It was a different kind.
If you eat the Bread that's *Me,* you will not die like them,
But you will live forever in a world that has no end."

Chapter 6:60-71

These words of Christ perplexed His friends, and His disciples said,
"We do not *really* understand this discourse about bread.
The things He said are difficult, so how could He expect
That anybody listening would follow or accept?"

Aware that they were grumbling, the Lord said in reply,
"If you think this is hard to grasp, you'd *really* wonder why
If I should say 'the Son of Man will soon be here no more,
Because He will ascend e're long to where He was before.'"

"I did not mean that *literally* My body you should eat.
I was speaking spiritually to say My flesh was meat.
You miss the point and profit not at all if you don't see
The deeper meanings that My words convey are *heavenly.*"

"In spite of all I've tried to say about the need for trust,
Some of you still don't believe or see that faith's a must."
For Jesus knew, right from the start, that some would turn away.
He also knew with certainty the one who would betray.

At *this* point, many leaving said, "We're following no more!
There's nothing here worth staying for —we're heading for the door."
Asked Jesus, turning towards the twelve, "Will you desert me too?
Will you conclude, as they have done, there's nothing here for you?"

Then Simon Peter answered Him, "Oh Lord, where would we go?
If there's a better option, I am certain I don't know.
Eternal life is Yours to give, You are God's Holy One
And we're not leaving, that's for sure. We're certain You're His Son!"

Christ replied, "There're twelve of you but one is not on board."
He spoke of Judas who would soon contract to sell the Lord.

Chapter 7:1-13

Because the leaders hated Him and fervently wished Him dead,
Jesus stayed out of Judea, traveling Galilee instead.
But the Feast of Tabernacles was a feast then drawing near,
And His brothers said to Jesus, "Tell us why You're staying here?"

"Don't You think You should be going to the feast with all the rest?
Public figures usually mingle with the crowds —we think it best.
Show Yourself and let them marvel at the miracles You do.
If You're really who You say You are then You should be there too."

His brothers actually didn't believe the Messiah's who He was.
O'er the years they'd laughed and teased Him, prompting pain without a cause.
"The time's not right for Me just now to go there," Jesus said.
"Not yet. I'll linger here awhile in Galilee instead."

"The world will never hate you since you're filled with it, you see.
But it hates Me with a passion, for I make it feel guilty.
That is why I must be careful, for My time is not yet come.
Go ahead and leave without Me. You don't grasp where I come from."

So His brothers left without Him, traveling in a caravan,
As the highways streamed with pilgrims, crowding roads from every land.
When the traffic had subsided and the din and dust was gone,
Jesus headed for the city of Jerusalem --alone.

Now at the Feast the Savior was the talk on every tongue
As everybody wondered, "Is He brave enough to come?"
Some declared, "He *is* a good man." Others cursed vehemently,
"He is only a deceiver! Nothing good's from Galilee."

Chapter 7:14-36

Halfway through the Feast the Savior in the temple court appeared.
Since the leaders sought to kill Him those who saw Him greatly feared.
But He spoke with bold assurance though the leaders ridiculed,
"How did this Man get such learning, having never been to school?"

Jesus answered, "What I'm teaching did not come from Me alone.
It was given Me from Heaven, from My Father's glorious throne.
Those who care to follow God's will, know for certain when I speak,
He is actually speaking through Me. There's no doubt for those who seek."

"Those who value fame and honor look for ways to self-promote.
But the One who seeks God's glory speaks the truth —you should take note.
You're dishonest since you claim the law of Moses to revere,
All the while you plot to kill Me, but your schemes I do not fear."

"You must be possessed by demons! Who is trying to take Your life?"
Said the leaders and those with them. "Your words only stir up strife!"
Jesus answered, "You are angry that a cripple I restored
On the Sabbath, and you're certain I transgressed God's Holy Word."

"Yet on Sabbath you think nothing of a child to circumcise.
Quit your judging by appearance. Try to see through Heaven's eyes.
Is it wrong to heal a cripple, who for years longed to be whole?
Are your hearts completely hardened? No compassion in your soul?"

At that point some of those watching questioned, "Isn't He the one
That the leaders wish to murder? Yet He stands there in the sun
And they do not raise a finger. Do they think the Christ is *He*?
We all know where *this* Man comes from. That could never, ever be!"

Jesus answered, "Yes, you know Me and you know the town I'm from.
But *that* wasn't My beginning and you don't know why I've come.
I was sent here by Another, One you do not really know.
But *I* know Him, and He sent Me, which is why I'm here below."

Then their anger overcame them. "Let's arrest Him now," said some.
But they laid no hand upon Him, for His time had not yet come.
And besides, there were believers in the crowd with faith in Him
Who said, "When the Christ is come, will He do more signs than this Man?"

Pharisees who heard them whisper told the priests and leaders then,
"We must send guards to arrest Him or He'll captivate all men."
Jesus understood their plotting. He knew what they sought to do.
And He said, "It's not much longer I'll remain down here with you."

"Very soon I'll be returning to the One who sent Me here.
You will seek but you'll not find Me. Yes, that time is very near.
I have told you that you really do not know where I am from.
To this place where I am going, you will not be able to come."

"Where's this place that He is going?" asked the leaders, tongue in cheek,
"Where He thinks we cannot find Him? Will He live among the Greeks?
What He's saying is quite puzzling —who He is and where He's from.
How mysterious that He tells us we can *look* but cannot come."

Chapter 7:37-52

At the closing of the Feast, and on the greatest day of all,
Jesus stood up in the crowd and they heard Him loudly call.

"If this pageant's left you empty and you thirst for something more,
If you come to *Me* I'll give you drink that satisfies for sure."

"All who trust in Me, I promise (as the Scripture makes so clear),
Will be filled with Living Water from within – that will endure."
He was speaking of the Spirit which they later would receive,
If they put their trust in Him and with their whole hearts did believe.

Some who'd heard the words He'd spoken, said with joy, "The time has come!
Surely this man is *the* prophet! He's the *Christ*, the Holy One!"
Others said, "You are mistaken! Christ must come from Bethlehem.
This man is a Galilean. The Messiah can't be Him!"

So the people were divided and they argued long and loud.
But no man laid a hand on Him in that unruly crowd.
And when the temple guards returned to those who'd sent them out,
The chief priests and the Pharisees began to rant and shout.

"Why haven't you returned with Him?" they raged with angry voice.
"We meant to but," the guards replied, "we didn't have a choice.
We intended to arrest Him, but we failed and it's because
No one else has ever spoken in the way that this Man does!"

"What you *mean* is He's deceived *you,*" said the leaders with a sneer.
"That's why you failed to do your job and bring the scoundrel here.
Have you noted not a single one of us believe in Him?
You've been duped, as has that whole crowd! You're all cursed and full of sin!"

"I'm surprised," said Nicodemus, looking at their angry faces,
"That you've overlooked our legal code which says in many places,
Not a soul can be convicted without hearings and a trial.
What you're doing is illegal. You have missed it by a mile!"

They replied, "Are you duped also? Are you too from Galilee?
If you'd thoroughly search the Scriptures, we are certain you would see
That no prophet ever comes from such a worthless place! It's clear!
You're completely uninformed and maybe don't belong in here."

Chapter 8:1-11

Just outside Jerusalem, there amid the groves of trees,
Jesus spent the night upon the Mount known as Olives.
But early the next morning He came back into the town
And sat down in the temple court with people gathered 'round.

Then right as He was teaching them, some teachers of the law,
Along with Pharisees approached and Jesus looking, saw
They'd brought a woman stripped and shamed. "Adultery," they said.
"We caught her in the very act and pulled her from the bed."

They placed her right in front of Him, surrounded by the crowd,
And then demandingly they spoke in tones both harsh and loud,
"Moses' law condemns this girl and says she should be stoned.
If You agree, we'll kill her *now.*" Then Jesus sighed and groaned.

The leaders actually didn't care at all about this girl.
It was a trap to snare the Lord. 'Twas Him they hoped to kill.
But Jesus didn't answer them. Instead He stooped to write
Words in the dust, revealing sins they'd hoped to hide from sight.

Then looking in their eyes He spoke. His words cut like a knife,
"Let those of you who're without sin be first to take her life."
Then stooping down, again He wrote, in dust with finger firm,
Exposing them for who they were, each leader in his turn.

Then one by one they slipped away ashamed that all could see
They were the ones who'd just been trapped in their hypocrisy.

And as they left -from old to young- the woman cowered there,
But Jesus knelt beside her while the crowd, dumbfounded, stared.

Then Jesus spoke and said to her, "Where are those who accused?"
His heart was grieved to see her pain and how she'd been abused.
The woman dared to look around, then said incredulously,
"Those who condemned have disappeared. You're all that's left with me."

"*I* don't condemn," the Savior said, "their words we will ignore!
You're free to leave. You've been forgiven. Now go, and sin no more."

Chapter 8:12-20

Then Jesus, speaking to the crowd, in words they'd long recall,
Said, "I'm the Light of this whole world. I blaze a path for all.
And if you follow Me," He said, "through good times or through strife,
You will not walk in darkness, for My light will lead to life."

Some Pharisees nearby replied, "Your claims cannot be true.
You're just boasting of Yourself and that You should not do."
In response the Savior said, "Though of Myself I spoke,
What I said is still the truth! You're trying to provoke."

"I *know* where I have come from and where I'm going too.
You really can't discredit Me. Discernment's not in you.
You presume to be My judge and look through human eyes.
Conclusions that you form are wrong and nothing more than lies."

"I don't judge but if I did, My judgment would be right,
Because the Father's with Me, though He's hid from earthly sight."

"Your laws say, if two agree their witness must be true.
With My words I've testified. My Father's spoken too."

"Where's Your Father?" they replied. "We've never seen *Him* here."
Jesus answered, "Nonetheless, beside Me He is near!
If you really knew the truth of My identity
Then My Father you'd know too, because He's just like Me."

They rebelled against His claim about where He was from.
But they did not arrest Him then. His hour had not yet come.

Chapter 8:21-30

Once again the Savior said, "I'll soon be going away.
And though you try to look for Me, and though you search all day,
You will not find Me. But instead, in sin you will succumb.
The place I will be going to is somewhere you can't come."

The Jews said to each other then, "What is this all about?
Does He plan to kill Himself? He's crazy! There's no doubt!
What's He mean, 'You cannot come?' To us it makes no sense."
Thus they spoke among themselves and thus they took offense.

But then the Lord continuing said, "You're from here below
And the things of which I speak are things that you can't know.
You are from this world for sure, that's why you don't perceive.
That I've come down from up above. You just will not believe."

"Unless you change the way you think and trust yourselves to Me,
Sadly, you will die in sin. The next world you'll not see."
They replied with sneers and scorn, "Who do You think You are?"
"I've told you plainly," Jesus said, "My words you just ignore."

"I have much to say to you and much that will condemn.
But I'll not speak of it just now. You'll hear Me in the end.
My Father gives Me what I speak. It's truth by Heaven sent."
The Jews just stood and stared at Him. They knew not what He meant.

Then Jesus said, "Eventually, you'll start to understand,
When on the cross you've lifted up and killed the Son of Man,
That I've done nothing on My own. I've taught what I was given
By My Father, who's with Me, though *He* is still in Heaven."

"What I do He has endorsed. He leaves me not alone."
Then many in the crowd believed and said, "He is the One!"

Chapter 8:31-59

To those who *did* believe Christ said, "You're Mine if you remain
Faithful to the things I've taught. Please listen, I'll explain.
My disciples know the truth which is what sets them free."
"What do You mean?" they answered Him. "On this we don't agree."

"We descend from Abraham and slaves we've never been."
Jesus answered, "That's not true, for you are slaves to sin.
And slaves, quite unlike children, are *not* the family.
But if the Son delivers you, then truly you are free."

"Technically I know you come from Abraham's family tree.
Yet even though I speak the truth, you're trying to kill Me.
And that's because you have no heart for what I say and teach.
But I speak what I've seen with God. He tells me what to preach."

"He's My father but He's not yours. You have a different one."
"*Our* father's Abraham," they said, "we've told you we're his sons!"
"If that were true," Christ answered, "you'd do what Abraham did.
And *he* would never want to kill Me for the things I've said."

"I'm a Man who's told you truth —things God has given Me.
No! Abraham is not your dad! It's someone else, I see."
"We're not illegitimate like You," the Jews replied.
"God's our father and what's more, we know He's on *our* side."

"*That* can't be," Christ answered them, "if it were true you'd love
The Son He's sent. For as I've said, I came down from above.
You cannot even understand the things I say —it's clear!
In fact it's even worse than that, you cannot even hear!"

"You're children of the devil and you love the things he does.
He is a murderer like you. In fact, he always was.
He has always hated truth. There is *no* truth in him.
He's a liar and a cheat —the father of all sin."

"That's why when *I* speak the truth, *you* choose to disbelieve.
Like your father satan, you just argue and deceive.
There's not a single one of you who can find sin in Me.
I am pure and speak the truth but you refuse to see."

"Those who are My Father's know and gladly hear My word.
The fact that you're not *His* explains the reason you've not heard."
In rage the Jews retorted then, "You are possessed for sure!
A demon from Samaria! We *know* that's what *You* are!"

"That's not true," the Savior said. "No demons will you see
Because *I* live to honor God —but *you* dishonor Me.
And though I've never had the wish Myself to glorify,
God *will* bring Me glory and *you'll* see it by and by."

"Listen, for I tell the truth, I promise," Jesus cried
"That those who will obey My words will live and never die."

The people said, "You've proved it now! By demons You're possessed!
Abraham's gone, the prophets too, they've died like all the rest.
And yet *You* promise endless life! Who *do* You think You are?
Someone above Abraham? Your teaching is bizarre!"

Jesus answered, "If I boast or *My*self glorify,
It wouldn't really mean a thing. So let Me verify.
My Father, whom you claim as yours, intends that I receive
Bright glory from His throne above —if only you'd believe."

"You don't know Him but I do, and if *that* I denied,
I'd be a liar just like you, but I am *not*," Christ cried.
"I'm telling you I know Him well and also keep His Word.
But though I've said it all before, it's something you've not heard."

"Your father Abraham rejoiced, and he was very glad
As he looked forward to My day —prophetic eyes he had."
The people answered sneeringly, "Whatever do You mean?
A half a century You've not lived, yet Abraham You've seen?"

Then Jesus answered and His words like thunder split the air.
"Before that patriarch was born, I was already there!
Repeatedly you have referred to Father Abraham,
But long before his time on earth, I Was because I AM!"

Then at that point they picked up stones. "Let's kill Him!" came their cries.
But Christ, like vapor vanishing, was hidden from their eyes.

Chapter 9:1-11

Once as Jesus walked along He saw a man born blind.
His disciples had a question that was troubling their minds.
The circumstances of his birth perplexed them, so they asked,
"Was his blindness caused by sins committed in the past?"

"Did his parents make mistakes or was it his own sin?
Was his blindness caused by something that was evil from within?"
"Not a chance!" the Savior said. "His parents weren't the cause.
Nor was his suffering the result of breaking any laws."

"But if you watch you'll see how God can turn a thing that's bad
Into a blessing, even though the problem is so sad.
Troubles come and troubles go. There is no end to strife,
But God displays His power through a damaged, broken life."

"While the sun's still shining, we must do the work of Him
Who has sent us on a mission to this broken world we're in.
The dark will soon be coming and it's hard to work at night.
But while I'm still here in this world, I'll blaze. I *AM* the Light!"

After having said these words, Christ spat upon the ground,
As His disciples, looking on, pressed close and gathered 'round.
Mixing spittle with some dirt, the way kids make mud pies,
He took the mud, applying it to the blind man's vacant eyes.

"Now go and wash in Siloam's pool," the Savior softly said.
So Christ's disciples took his hand and there the blind man led.
Then when he'd washed the mud away, his vision was restored
And Christ's disciples marveled at the power of the Lord.

The neighbors of the man born blind, when he had come home seeing,
Struggled to accept the fact that there had been a healing.
"Can this be the man we know who begged beside the street,
Doing what he could," they said, "to scrounge enough to eat?"

"No," said some, "he's not the man. He only looks the same.
We are sure that if you ask, he has a different name."
But the man himself declared, "Yes, it is really me!"
They asked him, disbelieving, "Tell us how it is you see?"

He replied "Well, Jesus put some mud upon my eyes,
Sent me to the pool to wash and much to my surprise,
For the first time I could see, and that's why I rejoice.
I'm so happy I must shout His praises with my voice."

Chapter 9:12-42

"Where is He?" his neighbors asked, "the One who gave you sight?"
"I don't know," the man replied while squinting at the light.
Then they took the man to see some Pharisees who said,
"This Man healed on Sabbath. Tell us everything He did!"

The one born blind responded, "He put mud upon my eyes.
When I'd washed them, all was different. I could see, to my surprise."
Then the leaders frowned and sputtered, "This Man broke our favorite rule,
For He healed upon the Sabbath —something God would never do!"

Some who stood by listening said, "Come on! How could *that* be?
Without the power of God no *sinner* causes blind to see!"
So a deep division rose as each expressed his view.
The Pharisees grew more concerned and fretted what to do.

Then they asked the man born blind to tell them what *he* thought
About the One who'd healed him, and such a wonder wrought.

"I think He is a prophet!" said the man emphatically.
The Jewish leaders answered, "You weren't blind! This cannot be!"

Then they summoned both his parents and they said, "Is this your son?
Would you lead us to believe that he's been blind since being born?
If you say that is the case, then kindly tell us now
When it was he came to see - and more precisely, *how*?"

His parents answered, "He's our son and he's been blind since birth.
But we don't know how all that changed. Ask *him*, for what it's worth.
He's certainly quite old enough to answer on his own.
Ask him again, if you can't grasp just how the thing was done."

His parents were evasive for the Jews had made it clear
They would punish Christ's supporters, so they had good cause to fear.
They could be expelled from worship in the synagogue, and so
They did not give their opinion then or let their feelings show.

A second time the Jews addressed the man who'd been born blind.
"*God* must get the glory here!" (They hoped to change his mind).
"This Man is a sinner and we know this to be true."
"Perhaps *you're* blind," replied the man, "I've got some news for you!"

"Whether He's a sinner man or whether He is not,
I'm not qualified to say but since you've put me on the spot,
One thing I know for certain: I was blind but now I see.
You are witnessing a miracle and it happens to be *me*."

Yet again the leaders asked him, "What exactly did He do?"
Said the man, "What is the problem? I have already told you!"
He continued, "What's the reason you would hear it all again?
The first time you didn't listen. Do you want to follow Him?"

Then they said, "*You're* His disciple!" And they cursed him yet again.
"Moses receives our allegiance, for we know God spoke to him.
But as for this imposter, who you claim has wonders done,
We don't even know His parents or the place where He is from."

"This is certainly amazing!" said the man with great surprise,
"That you don't know where He comes from, yet He opened up my eyes!
God won't listen to a sinner, that's a truth that's certain still!
But He *does* hear those who worship and who seek to do His will."

"No one *ever* has been able to restore sight to the blind.
You could search since time began and yet you'll never find
Someone who could do the things that He has done today.
Unless this man has come from God, to do this there's no way!"

"You were born a sinner!" said the leaders in a fuss.
"Who do you think you are that you could try to instruct us?"
Then they sent to fetch the guards and cast him from that place.
"You are banned from synagogues! Don't ever show your face!"

When the Savior heard about the things the leaders did,
He searched until He found that man and this is what He said.
"Do you trust the Son of Man? In Him do you believe?"
The man replied, "Who is He sir? I'd gladly Him receive!"

"You have seen Him," Jesus said, "He's speaking to you now."
"I believe, Lord!" said the man, and worshiped with a bow.
Then Christ said, "I came to earth to give the blind their sight,
And show the ones who think they see that they're not really right."

Some Pharisees were standing near and asked Christ, "Are *we* blind?"
Jesus answered, "If you were, God probably wouldn't mind.
But since you say that you can see and make pretentious claims,
I tell you this, you're guilty still and all your sin remains."

Chapter 10:1-21

"I tell you the truth," said Jesus. "A sheep pen has a door.
And those who try to climb the wall are thieves or robbers, sure.
The man who enters by the gate is shepherd of those sheep.
The watchman opens up for him when all the flock's asleep."

"The sheep will recognize his voice and follow him about.
They come and go at his request. His voice will lead them out.
He calls each sheep by its own name. They understand him well.
They follow not a stranger, for *his* voice they cannot tell."

"They always run away," said Christ, "from any stranger's voice.
This is a fact a shepherd knows. They follow him by choice."
The people who were listening just didn't understand.
They looked confused so Jesus tried explaining it again.

"I Am the Gate for all the sheep. There's never been another.
And all of those who came before were only thieves and robbers.
Happily, the sheep ignored those ones who came before,
And that is good, for as I've said, I AM the only Door."

"Those who through Me enter in, I promise will be saved.
But thieves just come to steal and kill and lay you in the grave.
I have come to give you life and that abundantly.
I AM the Good Shepherd and I *love* the sheep, you see."

"Good shepherds will lay down their lives if it could save a sheep.
The love they have for their whole flock is tender and so deep!
But hired hands will run away when wolves attack to kill.
'They're not *my* sheep,' they say as they go racing down the hill."

"I Am a *better* Shepherd for I will not run away.
My sheep know Me and I know them and with Me they will stay.
I also know the Father and He knows Me just as well.
And I will give My life to save the sheep who with Me dwell."

"And other sheep I have," said Christ, "for there are other pens.
And they all listen to My voice and through Me enter in.
For truth be known, there's just one flock, one Shepherd of them all.
No matter where they are I know they'll respond to My call."

"The Father loves Me all the more, because I will lay down
My life to save the flock one day, so *all* the lost are found.
I'll also take it up again. I have authority
To do this of My own accord. None take My life from Me!"

At these words the Jews were split. "He is possessed!" some said.
"Why listen to a fool like this? He's gone completely mad!"
But others said, "That's just not true! How can one who's possessed
Restore the sight of one born blind? We think He is the best!"

Chapter 10:22-42

Now to the Dedication Feast held in Jerusalem,
(Which happens every winter there), the Savior chose to come.
He walked into the temple grand, the porch of Solomon,
Where Jews surrounded Him and said, "Please say if You're the One."

"Don't keep us wondering, doubting, but tell us clear and plain.
We want to know for sure if You are true or are insane."
Jesus said, "I've told you all but you will not believe.
The works My Father's done through Me, you never do receive."

"The truth is you are not My sheep! As I have said to you -
My sheep respond and follow Me, but this *you* will not do.
I know My sheep and they know Me. Rich life to them I give.
And they will never perish but forevermore shall live."

"There's one more thing I want to say, while in this court I stand,
The ones I'm holding onto? None can snatch them from My hand!
My Father who has given them to Me is greater still!
None can pull them from *His* hand and no one ever will!"

"You need to understand," said Christ, "the Father and the Son -
These two of whom I spoke just now- are actually truly One!"
At that the Jews all picked up stones. "He has to die!" they said.
But Jesus asked, "Which of My works has made you want me dead?"

They answered, "It is not for works or things that You have done,
But rather that a Man like You would claim to be God's Son."
Jesus said, "It's in your Law, 'I've said that you are gods.'
If that is so, please tell Me now, what problem does this cause?"

"I'm only quoting Scripture that applies to every man.
And you know it is written there! Why can't you understand?
It really isn't blasphemy for God's own Son to say
That He's divine. How could you think it any other way?"

"Don't believe Me if I don't do what My Father does.
But if I *do* work miracles, you should believe because
The Father *has* to be in Me and I in Him as well!
How else can you explain My works? If they're not His, please tell?"

Again they tried to seize Him and again He slipped away.
He went down by the Jordan where the Baptist used to stay.
And many followed, saying, "Mighty works John did not do,
But all he said about *this* Man has come completely true!"

So Jesus lingered in that place where He was well received.
And many who had followed Him declared that they believed.

Grand And Glorious

Chapter 11:1-44

A man named Lazarus was quite sick. He lived in Bethany
In a home with sisters two, named Martha and Mary.
This Mary is the one who poured perfume upon Christ's feet.
And Martha was the cook who made Him scrumptious meals to eat.

When Lazarus became ill the girls to Christ a message sent.
"Your friend is very sick," they wrote, and this is what they meant:
Because we know You care for us and don't forget Your friends,
We believe You will respond and soon this illness end.

When Jesus heard, He sent reply, "Your brother will not die.
This happened for God's glory and you'll see it by and by."
So although Jesus loved them and their sorrow made Him sad,
With His disciples He remained for two days more, then said,

"Let's head for Judea now." But His friends responded, "No!
Recently they sought to *kill* You. It's not wise to go!"
Jesus answered, "It's OK to walk when it is light.
People need not fear unless they're walking in the night."

"Lazarus is now asleep, but it is My intent
To wake our friend from slumber deep with life that's Heaven sent."
Christ's disciples answered Him, "Lord, if he's sleeping now,
He'll be getting better soon. This trip we can't allow."

Jesus' words they did not grasp, nor did they understand,
That what Christ meant was, "He is dead, and we're not close at hand."

So He told them plainly then, "Our friend has passed away.
And I am glad I was not there, but we are going *today*."

Christ's disciples lingered still; they did not want to leave.
But Jesus said, "Once we return, I tell you, you'll believe!"
Thomas, who was called the Twin, said, "Well then let us go.
If He is going to die I want to die with Him also."

When they got to Bethany, the mourners let them know,
"Lazarus lies within in his grave —interred four days ago."
Bethany's just down the road, quite near Jerusalem.
And many who were there to grieve from that place had just come.

Some of them brought Martha word that Jesus was outside.
So she went out to meet Him then and when she saw Him cried,
"Lord, if You had just been here, my brother would be well.
But God will give You anything You ask now, even still."

Jesus said, "He'll rise again. He has not gone to stay."
Martha answered, "Yes, I know. He'll rise on *judgment* day."
"I am Resurrection and I'm Life as well," Christ said.
"Those who trust in Me may *die*. But they're not *truly* dead."

"To all who live and trust in Me I give eternal life.
Do you believe Me when I say there'll be an end to strife?"
"Yes, Lord," Martha answered, "I believe You are God's Son.
And that you came to this world so that His will might be done."

After this she went to tell her sister Christ had come
And that He'd asked to see her too. She took off on a run.
The Jews who had been comforting the sisters saw her leave,
And so they followed to the tomb, expecting there to grieve.

When Mary reached where Jesus was, she weeping prostrate fell,
And at His feet she sobbing said, "My brother'd be here still
If You had only been here Lord - he never would have died.
Oh Jesus, if You'd only come!" there at His feet she cried.

When Jesus saw her anguished form and heard the mourners moan,
His heart was deeply troubled and He answered with a groan,
"Please show Me where you've laid him, and where his body's kept."
Then tears fell from the Savior's eyes, as with them all He wept.

Some said, "How He loved him!" While others sneered and frowned,
"He could heal a blind man but He's let this family down!"
"Come and see," still others said and led Christ to the tomb.
It was sealed, so Jesus said, "Please roll away the stone."

"But *Lord*!" cried Martha in distress, "the odor will be foul!
He's been lying there four days! He's decomposing now!"

Jesus answered, "Didn't I say, if only you'd believe,
The glory of God would be revealed? This you are going to see."
So they rolled away the stone and Jesus prayed out loud,
"God, I know You hear Me but I'm saying this for the crowd."

"What I am requesting now is for their benefit.
I want them to believe the truth, that I'm the One You've sent."
And after He had prayed this, Jesus spoke in a loud voice,
"Lazarus come forth right now! Let's see this crowd rejoice!"

Then from deep within the tomb there came a rustling sound.
Lazarus stepped out from that grave, in linens tightly bound.
"Unwrap him and let him go," the Savior did command,
And news of what He did that day spread all across the land!

Chapter 11:45-57

Many of those gathered 'round believed when they saw this.
But some ran to the Pharisees, who, not to be remiss,
Summoned the Sanhedrin then. "What shall we do?" they said.
"This Man keeps working miracles and now He's raised the dead!"

"If we don't put a stop to this, the world will follow Him!
And we'll not only lose our place, we'll lose our whole nation."
"You are fools!" Caiaphas said --he was High Priest that year.
"You do not see we have no choice! It's all so very clear!"

"This Man must die, or all will lose their country and their home.
A major insurrection will be crushed for sure by Rome.
It's come to this," Caiaphas said, "if this Man doesn't die,
Our nation will just perish and *we'll* be the reason why."

He actually didn't say this on his own, but prophesied,
That Christ's death would be for the Jews and all the world besides.
Then from that day they plotted how to take the Savior's life,
By stones or crucifixion or by hanging or by knife.

So Jesus ceased to mingle and to move among the Jews.
Departing for the wilderness, He quietly slipped from view.
The Passover was drawing near and many pilgrim bands
Traveled to Jerusalem from near and distant lands.

They each one talked of Jesus and they hoped to see Him there.
"Will He come?" they whispered, while looking everywhere.
Meanwhile the Sanhedrin court had issued a decree:
Anyone seeing Jesus must report – immediately!

Chapter 12:1-11

Just six days before Passover, Jesus came to Bethany.
That's the town of His friend Lazarus, who'd been dead as dead could be.
He attended there a dinner where He was the honored guest.
Martha catered the occasion since her cooking was the best.

Mary brought a pound of spikenard, costly oil for Jesus' feet,
Which she poured with love upon Him as the guests reclined to eat.
All attending quickly noticed as the fragrance filled the air.
Mary, weeping, kissed His feet and wiped them with her hair.

The disciple known as Judas - the betrayer - filled with rage
Said, "That spikenard's worth a fortune and could sell for a year's wage."
He, pretending to be thoughtful, claimed concern for all the poor,
Saying, "What a waste to spend so much for oil spilt on the floor."

"If only she had given that much money to our cause,
I'd have seen that it was shared with needy boys and girls."
But though he sounded pious, Jesus saw through his disguise.
He'd have stolen from the purse they kept to pay for their supplies.

"Leave her be," the Savior said, "she was saving that perfume.
It was intended for my burial but instead it fills this room.
She alone has understood. That's why she's honoring Me.
The poor of which you speak, when I am gone, will always be."

A crowd had formed outside the place while they'd been eating there.
They hoped to see the Savior and at Lazarus get to stare.
So the chief priests, who'd been planning soon to see the Savior dead,
Concluded, "Lazarus too must die. He turns too many heads."

Chapter 12:12-19

The next day news swept through the crowd, who'd gathered for the Feast,
That Jesus was Jerusalem bound - and riding on a beast!
So with joy they gathered branches, waving palms along the way,
And they lined the streets while shouting, "Now at last, *this* is the day!"

And they offered God glad praises, saying, "Blessed is the One
Who's arriving in the Lord's name. Hail! The King of Israel's come!"
They recalled the words of prophets who had said, long years ago,
Israel's king would enter riding upon a donkey's foal.

(His disciples, who'd forgotten that this entry'd been foretold,
After He'd been glorified recalled those words of old.)
But the crowd continued shouting and they filled the air with song,
While the priests and rulers muttered, "After Him the whole world's gone!"

Chapter 12:20-50

Now some Greeks, who'd come to worship, sought out Philip with request,
"Sir," they said, "we would see Jesus. We have heard that He's the best!"
Philip shared their words with Andrew then they both to Jesus went,
Telling Him about the Greeks and the message they had sent.

Christ appeared as lost in thought, then quietly He replied,
"The hour has come. The Son of Man will soon be glorified.
One thing's for sure - unless a grain of wheat falls to the ground,
And buried there, appears to die, no harvest will be found."

"The man on earth who loves his life and lives for self alone,
Will find at last, on judgment day, no Savior shall atone.
But those who live for others and to self they pay no mind,
Will gain the most while living here - and life forever find."

"All who serve are followers and where I Am they'll be.
My Father loves to honor those who've chosen to love Me.
But now My heart is troubled. Evil's pressing with its power.
What shall I say? 'Oh Father, please release Me from this hour?'"

"That will *not* be My response! No! This is why I came!
Father, I will not draw back. Please glorify Your name."
Then thunder rolled from and up above it was heard by men.
"I've glorified it once," God spoke, "I'll do the same again!"

The crowd responded, "What was that? Are angels overhead?"
"It was for your benefit, not Mine," the Savior said.
"Satan fancies he's the prince of this world, but he's not.
He's about to be cast out. In his own trap he's caught."

"But I, when I am lifted up, will draw all men to Me,"
Christ said, to show the kind of death He'd die upon a tree.
The crowd asked, "Who's this 'Son of Man' who must be lifted high?
The Christ remains forever, yet You say You're going to die?"

Jesus answered, "Listen well! You're almost out of light.
And it will not be long before you're walking in the night.
Those who're walking in the dark don't know where they are going.
Trust the Light while there's still time and walk the path it's showing."

After this the Savior left and hid Himself from them.
In spite of all His miracles, they wouldn't trust in Him.
Of them Isaiah wrote when he asked, "God, who has believed?
The message that revealed the Lord, these folks have not received."

"For God's bright Light has blinded them and deadened their hard hearts.
They cannot see or understand. With Him they'll have no part."
Yet at the same time there were some, though leaders they might be,
Who did believe but followed not, because of Pharisees.

They were afraid they'd be cast out. They loved the praise of men.
So they did not confess their faith in Christ but denied Him.
Then with a loud voice Jesus cried, "Those who believe in Me
Also believe in God as well, for we're the same, you see."

"I have come into this world to be a light that shines,
So those who do believe in Me, a path through darkness find.
But as for those who listen, yet refuse to keep My word,
I did not come to judge them —no matter what you've heard."

"I did not come to judge the *world*. I came to save instead.
But nonetheless there'll come a time for judgment," Jesus said.
"And those who choose to not respond will their own selves condemn.
The time that they are given now, will then come to end."

"Remember that I told you, I'm not speaking on My own.
The Father, Who has sent Me, told Me what He wants made known.
Listen and apply these words and you will live forever
With Me in God's heavenly home where we will be together."

Prayers And Promises

Chapter 13:1-17

Just before Passover's Feast, His time now running out,
Jesus knew this world He'd leave - quite soon, without a doubt.
The Father once again He'd see, His mission then complete.
But first, to show how much He loved, He knelt to wash some feet.

The evening meal was being served and Judas, full of sin,
Had plans in place to sell the Lord, and basely betray Him.
Jesus knew that He'd received all power from His Father.
And though He'd be returning soon, He filled a bowl with water.

Removing first His outer clothes, He wrapped a towel around.
His friends observed with disbelief and didn't make a sound.
He washed their feet and dried them too. He served them one by one -
Until He came to Peter, who believed He was God's Son.

"Oh Lord, You *cannot* wash my feet," said Peter in protest.
He so respected Jesus that he did not think it best.
Jesus answered, "At this time, you do not understand.
But later I am sure you will begin to comprehend."

"Not a chance!" Peter replied. "You'll never wash my feet!"
Jesus said, "If I do not, you'll have no part with Me."
"If *that* is so, not just my feet but wash my hands and head.
I cannot bear to lose You Lord," Peter in anguish said.

Jesus answered, "Those who've bathed need only wash their feet.
Their bodies are still clean and they're just sitting down to eat."

"Now all of you are clean but one." Christ knew who would betray,
And that it would be Judas who would soon be on his way.

Then after He had finished and put on His robe again,
Jesus softly questioned, "Do you think you understand?
You call Me Lord and Master and your words are very true.
What I've done was an example and I gave it just for you."

"As you know, no servant's greater than the master he works for.
The same is true for messengers who only serve their lord.
Please make the application. My example I have given.
For when you're serving you will find that you are blest by Heaven."

Chapter 13:18-38

Jesus mentioned to His friends a fulfilled prophecy:
"One of you, who shares My bread, will place his heel on Me.
Before it's actually happened, I have told you so you'll know
That I've fulfilled the Scriptures, and then you'll believe that's so."

"Now also in the future please know that this is true:
Those who receive the ones I send, receive and love Me too.
And those who do accept Me, accept My Father as well.
For He's the One who sent Me and with Him I once did dwell."

After having said these things, Christ spoke with troubled heart,
"One of you will betray Me. I've known this from the start."
Stunned and shocked with disbelief, His friends all looked around,
Wondering who the traitor was and if he could be found.

Then Peter motioned to the one who next to Christ reclined.
(The one whom Christ kept loving still, though he was unrefined).
"Ask Him who He means," and so that loved disciple said,
"Lord please tell who'd do this thing while with You sharing bread?"

Jesus said, "I'll give him bread that I've dipped in this cup,
And he will absentmindedly receive and eat it up."
Then to Judas Christ did hand the morsel dipped in sauce,
And Satan entered into him —for he was Judas' boss.

"What you intend to do," Christ said, "go now and please be quick."
(He was the one who'd joined their group, that Jesus did *not* pick).
So Judas left but none of those remaining in the room
Understood what Christ had said -till He was in the tomb.

Since Judas was their treasurer, they thought he'd left to buy
More provisions for the Feast, which were in short supply.
But they were sorely incorrect, their thinking wasn't right.
And Judas, Christ's betrayer, slipped away into the night.

After he'd gone out to do that horribly evil deed,
Jesus said, "You know I Am the Son of Man indeed.
And what's about to happen will both shock and horrify!
But don't despair, God will be there, the Son to glorify."

"My children, I am only here with you a short time more.
And though you look you'll not find Me, the way you have before.
For as I told the Jews, I will return to where I'm from.
The place where I am going to, right now you cannot come."

"One last thing I leave with you, it is a new command:
Love each other as I've loved you and all will understand
That you are My disciples, for that kind of love is rare.
Wherever it occurs they'll know that I Am also there."

Simon Peter said, "Oh Lord, where is it You will go?
I intend to follow You and so I need to know."
"You can't follow Me right now," the Savior made reply.
"But you will follow later, though just now I can't tell why."

Peter said, "I'll follow now! I'll give my life for You."
Jesus answered, "That sounds good but this is what is true:
Before the rooster crows at dawn, you will have thrice denied
That you have ever known Me, friend," the Savior sadly sighed.

Chapter 14:1-14

"But Peter, don't you worry, I'm about to tell you why.
I'll be working on a house for you — you'll see it by and by.
You can trust in God for certain. You can trust in Me also.
And if that really wasn't true, I would have told you so."

"In this place where I am going there are many mansions fair.
And if I go to build them, I will come to take you there.
My Home would just feel empty if My friends weren't there with Me.
Which is why I'll come and get you. Where I Am you too will be."

"Now if you've paid attention to the things that I have said,
Then you'll know without a question how to reach what lies ahead."
"Lord, we *don't* know where You're going so how will we find the way?"
Questioned Thomas, sounding doubtful, for he knew not what to say.

Jesus answered, "Let Me tell you, I'm the Truth, the Life, the Way.
Not a soul comes to the Father unless in Me they stay.
If you really knew Me as you can, you'd know My Father too.
Since you do know Me, you do know Him. We are in this just for you."

Philip said, "Show us the Father. That'll be enough for me."
Jesus answered, "Come now Philip! Can you really still not see?
After how long I've been with you? After all that I have done?
How can you yet not understand the Father and I are one?"

"Even the *words* I say to you, I've not said on My own.
And all the *works* you've seen came from My Father — Him alone.
Believe the Father is in Me and I am in Him too!
But if that still you can't accept, believe the works I do."

"Since all those works were done by Him, another thing is true:
You can also do such works when He's living in you.
In fact, you will do greater things than these in days ahead,
Because I'm going to be with Him — but those we'll leave unsaid."

"Yes, you can ask for anything, if you ask in My name,
And I'll do it to glorify My Father," Christ exclaimed.

Chapter 14:15-31

"If you love Me you will find obedience results,
Because your heart becomes like Mine and in My law exults.
I'm going to ask My Father to send a special Gift.
The Holy Spirit is His name. You won't be left adrift."

"And He will bring you comfort. He will also lead you well.
The world cannot receive Him. They would rather 'buy and sell.'
But you aren't unfamiliar with this Friend of Whom I speak.
You've learned to recognize Him, for He dwells in those who're meek."

"No, I will not abandon you as orphans with no home.
I'll come along beside you and you'll never walk alone.
The world just won't be able to see Me anymore.
But you will see Me ever as you open your heart's door."

"When I'm raised to life again, united we will be.
I'll be in the Father and my friends will be in Me.
I've told you how that love results in keeping My commands.
It is the *only* way you can do what My Law demands."

"Those who seek Me know My love. My Father loves them too.
And We'll reveal ourselves to them. It's something that We do."
Then Judas (not the traitor) asked, "Will we alone see You?"
Jesus answered, "Those who love will see what We *both* do."

"They will do all that We say, and We will come to them,
And make their hearts our dwelling place. There Heaven will begin.
What I've said comes from Above. It's by My Father sent.
I've told you while I'm still with you, so you'll know what *He* meant."

"But when the Father sends to you the Holy Advocate,
He'll remind of all I've said, so you cannot forget.
Another gift I'm leaving you is peace of mind and heart.
The world will try to give the same, but it can't even start."

"So do not be troubled and don't ever be afraid.
Remember all I've told you and your fears will be allayed.
I'm returning to our God Who's greater than I am,
But I promise I'll be back to see you once again."

"These things I've tried to tell you before they come to pass,
So you'll believe when they unfold, and understand at last.
I don't have much more left to say. The enemy's drawing near.
He has no power over Me, so you don't need to fear!"

"My love for God compels Me and I want the world to know
I always do what He requires. But come, it's time to go."

Chapter 15:1-17

Jesus said, "I am the Vine —the only one that's true.
My Father is the Gardener and He knows just what to do.
He removes the branches on the Vine that don't bear fruit,
But those that are productive He will prune, and weeds uproot."

"You've been pruned and purified by what you've learned from Me.
Remain in Me and there'll be fruit that everyone can see.
A branch that's severed from the vine, no fruit will ever bear.
So stay in Me. I'll stay in you, and you will grow from there."

"Apart from Me, you'll nothing do. You'll be a branch that's dead.
And branches of that kind are burned —becoming fuel instead.
But if you will abide in Me and My words stay in you,
You can ask for anything and I will grant it too!"

"For when you bear a lot of fruit, My Father's glorified.
As others see the things you've done, *His* work can't be denied.
I've loved you like My Dad loves Me —you know it's just the same.
So may it always ever be, in My love you'll remain."

"There's something great that happens when you long abide in Me:
Obedience results in fruit. It happens naturally!
I've told you this so you'll be filled with joy from God above.
And also love each other in the way that I have loved."

"I tell you sure, no greater love has any man than this:
That he'd lay down his life to save those who are friends of his."

"You are the ones who've heard My words and followed what I've said.
You're not My slaves or servants. I have called you friends instead."

"You know you didn't choose Me but I have chosen you,
And appointed you to produce fruit —which you are going to do.
The Father's interested in this --He'll give you what you ask.
Remember *Love* is My command. It should be your first task."

Chapter 15:18-27

"You'll probably not be popular with those who're of the earth.
They hated Me, they'll hate you too. That does not change your worth.
A slave is never greater than his Master, it's a fact.
And since they persecuted Me, expect to be attacked."

"If they'd listened to the things I said, they'd listen to you too.
But if they choose to disregard, there's nothing you can do.
There's a reason they behave like this and it is all because
They do not know the One who sent Me to reveal His love."

"If I had not spoken to them, they wouldn't be guilty.
But now they've no excuse because they have rejected Me.
He who hates Me hates the Father since we are the same,
And I did all the things I did to represent His name."

"They've seen the wonders I have done throughout the year -each season.
They are fulfilling Scripture since they hate Me without reason."

"I've told you of the Counselor, God's Spirit and your Friend.
I'll send Him and He'll testify My love is without end.
And you must *also* testify, since you have been with Me.
The things you have experienced, I want the world to see."

Chapter 16:1-16

"These things I've said, I told you so your faith you won't let go.
They will expel and kill you since the Father they don't know.
They will be so much deluded they will think that God approves,
And even that they're serving Him with killing and abuse."

"Please remember I have warned you and I've told you in advance.
There's a devil out to get you. This won't happen just by chance."

"The One Who sent Me beckons, so I am about to leave.
You don't ask Me where I'm going but instead you only grieve.
Still it's best for you I'm leaving. If I don't, you'll never get
The Comforter I have talked about Who'll be your Advocate."

"And when *He* comes He will convict the world of mortal sin.
He'll also speak of righteousness and judgment in the end.
He'll help you see 'to sin' is *not* what most men thought it meant,
But rather it's not trusting in the One whom God has sent."

"See, righteousness is yours because I'm going to the Father,
Where I will plead My blood for you and Satan cannot bother.
He's coming up for judgment and will surely be condemned
To receive the sentence that's in fact already passed on him."

"I have still many things to say that you can't bear right now.
But when the Spirit comes, He'll guide and He will teach you how
To comprehend the things that I, while with you, left unsaid.
And He'll direct the very thoughts you have inside your head."

"He's like a funnel focusing things that are pouring through.
He'll share with you what He's received and show what's future too."
"All that the Father has is Mine. I oversee all things.
So when the Spirit gives to you, to Me it glory brings."

Chapter 16:16-33

"It won't be long before," said Christ, "that I'll be gone from view.
But shortly after that you'll see that I'll return to you."
The confused disciples questioned, "What ever does He mean?
What is it He is telling us, and why won't He be seen?"

Jesus said, "It's clear to Me that you would like to know
What I was referring to when I said I must go.
The truth is you will weep and mourn —though the world will rejoice.
But all your grief will be transformed and you will hear My voice."

"You could compare it to a woman when she's laboring to give birth.
She feels the pain and suffering, but later knows its worth.
So you'll experience sorrow now, but I'll see you again!
And after that the joy you have can't be removed by men."

"When all these things I'm speaking of have finally come to pass,
You'll find that you can go to God with things you want to ask.
And when you do, He'll grant requests you make using My name.
You'll connect directly with Him. Things will not be the same."

"I know I've talked with symbols but I'm going to tell you plain:
Things really will be different when you're asking in My name!
The Father loves you very much because you all love Me.
And He'll delight to grant requests because of that, you see."

"By the Father I was sent to come into this world.
I came to show you what He's like, His banner to unfurl.
The time is almost over now and I will soon return.
But you're aware that He's your Friend! Yes, you've begun to learn."

"Do you think you understand and do you now believe?
I'm trying to help you grasp the fact that I am soon to leave.
And you will each be scattered as you turn to run and flee,
But I will not be left alone. My Father's still with Me."

"I've told you this so you can have true peace in spite of trial.
When things go bad, I promise you, you'll still have strength to smile."

"The devil will attack and hurt in hopes that you'll succumb,
But do not fear. I've conquered him! The *world* I've overcome!"

Chapter 17:1-26

As He turned His eyes toward Heaven, the Savior said a prayer.
"Father, now we're getting closer to the *reason* I am here.
And I'm asking for this favor, that You'll glorify the Son,
So that I can bring You honor for the things that You have done."

"You have given Your Son power - absolute authority -
To decide the final outcome of each man's destiny.
He dispenses life eternal to each person who is saved
And He promises to raise each one that's resting in their grave."

"It's a gift that they are given when they know the One You've sent,
(And they come to know *You* also —both of Us, is what I meant.)
For We're about relationship, and love them to the core
When they hear us gently knocking and they open their heart's door."

"I've made sure I gave You glory by completing all the work
That You gave me to accomplish. Not one duty did I shirk.
So would You please restore Me to the glory I once had
When I dwelt with You in Heaven and in majesty was clad."

"You have softened many hearts here and You've given them to Me.
And I've revealed You to them, that Your glory they might see."

"They know all I have is Yours and that it's come from Heaven above.
They've accepted all I've taught them and they know that You are Love."

"I'm not praying for the world now but for those You've given Me,
For You know *I'm* soon departing, but *they* earthbound still will be.
Oh My Father please protect them by the power of Your name,
That they'll always be united, as we are, the very same."

"While on earth I've kept them sheltered. I have shielded them from pain
And I haven't lost a one - except for he that Satan claims.
Very soon I'll be returning. I can't wait to see You there!
But while here, I've shared Your joy and they know nothing can compare."

"The world has little use for them, for they don't belong to it.
They are living now for Heaven and the Spirit's made them fit.
I'm not asking that You take them from the world in which they live
But I'm asking, while they stay here, Your protection You will give."

"They do not belong to this world. They are just here passing through.
Make them holy through Your Scriptures as you teach to them Your truth.
In the way that You have sent Me, to this world I'm sending them,
And I pledge Myself that they might be made holy —free from sin."

"Not alone for My *disciples*, but for all who through them hear,
Is this prayer, Oh Holy Father, that You'd also hold *them* near.
It's My wish that *they* would also be united as We are.
So the world will know You sent Me, may they shine bright as a star."

"I want them so united in a fellowship of love
That the world will know this all came from their Father Who's above.
And I'm asking for the future, that to Me each one You've given
May at last be rescued and with Us live there in Heaven."

"Then they will see My glory in that Heaven where We'll dwell.
And they'll see how much You love Me - *they* will feel Your love as well.
Though the world just doesn't know You, Father, these disciples do.
That is because You sent Me and because I revealed You."

Sacrifice And Triumph

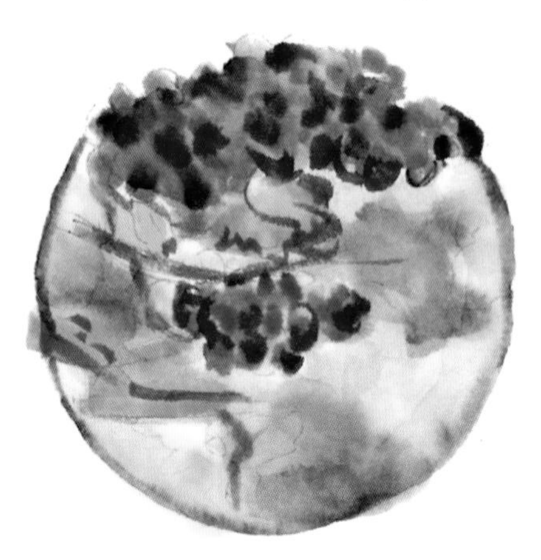

Chapter 18:1-11

Then when He'd finished praying, Jesus went across the brook
That is in the Kidron Valley, and with Him His friends He took.
And there with His disciples, in a grove of olive trees,
Jesus cried out to His Father as He knelt down on His knees.

Now Judas, who'd betrayed Him, knew the place where He'd be found
Since He'd often spent the night there as they slept upon the ground.
So he brought a band of soldiers with some priests and Pharisees.
They were carrying swords and torches as they moved in through the trees.

But Jesus fully realized all that soon would come to pass,
As He stepped out towards the soldiers and this question He did ask,
"Who have you come here looking for and what do you plan to do?"
"Jesus, Who's from Nazareth," said the soldiers. "Is that You?"

"I Am *He*," said Jesus boldly, to the mob gathered around.
And they all, along with Judas, tumbled prostrate to the ground.
As they cowered there in terror, Jesus asked a second time,
"Who have you come here searching for and hoping you would find?"

"The Nazarene, known as Jesus," they responded timidly.
"Just a moment back I told you," answered Jesus. "I Am He.
Since I'm the One you're looking for there's something you must know;
You may take Me where you want but you must let these others go!"

This He said fulfilling Scriptures that were written long ago
By inspired men and prophets, whom in vision God did show,

That the Christ would be triumphant and would say, despite the cost,
"That of all those I've been given, not a single one I've lost."

Then the one called Simon Peter, who was known for being rash,
Grabbed a sword and quickly struck off Malchus' ear with just one slash.
But the Savior said to Peter, "You must put your sword away!
Suffering's cup the Father gave Me I intend to drink today."

Chapter 18:12-27

Then the temple guards and soldiers, who had come for Christ's arrest,
Tightly bound His hands and took Him to the home of lord Annas.
He had been the former High Priest, but his son-in-law now ruled
The Sanhedrin, after having been by Annas thoroughly schooled.

He's the one known as Caiaphas, who to them had earlier said,
"It is better for our people we make sure this Man is dead!
He is gaining such a following and creating such a stir,
Rome will soon destroy our nation —and of that you can be sure."

Simon Peter followed Jesus at a distance, holding back.
When they reached the High Priest's palace, he an entry pass did lack.
But one more of Christ's disciples, whom Caiaphas also knew,
Was permitted entrance to the yard and spoke for Peter too.

So the woman who controlled the gate let Simon go on in.
But she said, as he was passing, "You're a *follower* of that Man."
"No!" Peter quickly answered, "I am not! That is *not* so!"
Then he stood beside the fire, since the night was very cold.

Meanwhile Annas questioned Christ about what He had taught.
"I've spoken in the open and in secret I've said naught,"
Said Jesus to Lord Annas, whom Christ's life presumed to seek.
"Why ask *Me* what I have said? Ask those who heard Me speak."

A temple guard heard Christ's response and struck Him on the head.
"Is that the way You answer the high priest?" he hotly said.
"If I said something wrong," Christ said, "please tell me what it was?
But if I didn't, *you* were wrong to strike without a cause."

Annas sensed those looking on could tell he had no case
So he sent Christ to Caiaphas, in order to save face.
And then the Savior, tightly bound, was hustled off again.
But *He* kept calm in spite of all the rough and angry men.

Meanwhile, in the courtyard, Simon Peter warmed his hands
Beside the crackling fire, mingling with the servant band.
One of them said, "You were *with* Him, His disciple's what you are."
"I am NOT!" responded Peter, as he stepped back from the fire.

But a man who was related to the one who'd lost his ear
Said, "I saw you in the garden. When they caught Him, I was near."
"You're a fool!" responded Peter, and he swore, "you do not know!
You mistake me for another!" Then he heard a rooster crow.

Chapter 18:28-40

Then from Caiaphas Christ was led to yet another place.
The Roman procurator was to meet Him face to face.
It was early in the morning and the Jews would not go in
To the palace of the governor and be "defiled by sin."

They were soon to eat Passover and they needed to stay pure,
So Pilate had to come outside and meet them where they were.
Disturbed from being wakened out of sleep, the governor asked,
"What are your accusations? And you'd better make it fast!"

"What charges are you bringing? Tell me what did this Man do?"
They replied, "If He weren't evil, we would not have come to you.
He is a criminal through and through, a scoundrel and a cheat.
We're certain you'll know what to do. We lay Him at your feet."

But Pilate said, "Take Him yourselves and judge Him by *your* law.
Your squabbles I'll not entertain. I'm going to withdraw."
The Jews said, "We can't execute and this Man has to die!"
(They failed to realize Jesus' death was actually prophesied.)

Then Pilate summoned Christ inside and asked with tongue-in-cheek,
"Are You the king of all the Jews? If so, I'll hear You speak."
Jesus said, "Why do you ask? Do you desire to know?
Or have you heard Me talked about and doubt that it is so?"

"Am I a Jew?" the governor sneered. "You matter not to me!
Your people and Your chief priests brought You here for me to see.
So tell me, what it is You've done that stirs their anger so?
I do not care, but I'm Your judge and so I need to know."

"My kingdom is not of this world," the Savior gave reply.
"My servants *would* fight if it were —to *win* they'd even die.
My kingdom's from another place and for another time.
You need not worry I'll attack. Your kingdom isn't Mine."

"So You're a king then?" Pilate said, "and yet You look forlorn?"
"I AM a King!" the Savior said. "This *is* why I was born.
I came to teach the world the truth —to make it crystal clear.
And those who value truth will know. They'll listen and they'll hear."

"What is truth?" the governor asked, and went back out again
To tell the people he could find no crime or guilt in Him.
But then he made an offer hoping that it would appease.
"We have a custom. I propose a prisoner to release."

"I'll offer you Barabbas as the prisoner you could choose,
Or this Jesus Who's from Nazareth and is King of all the Jews."
Then in a flash the mob roared back, to Pilate's disbelief,
"Not *Him*! Give us Barabbas!" —an assassin and a thief.

Chapter 19:1-16

So Pilate had Christ beaten till His back was torn to shreds.
Some soldiers made a crown of thorns and placed it on His head.
They took a ragged purple cloak and wrapped it all around,
Then mockingly they worshiped Him by bowing to the ground.

"All hail the King," they laughed and jeered, "Who rules across the land,"
While they both slapped and pounded Him with fist and open hand.
Then Pilate brought Him out and cried, "Behold this Man, right here!
I find in Him no fault at all. You've misjudged! It is clear!"

The Savior stood there regal-like, in spite of cloak and crown.
And though the crowd like lions roared, *He* didn't make a sound.
Once again the Governor said, "Behold Him with your eyes."
The crowd cried back vehemently, "Let Him be crucified!"

Pilate replied, "You take Him then, and do what you will do.
But I have found no fault in Him, and so the guilt's on you."
"Our law demands His death," they cried, "He calls Himself 'God's Son.'
We want Him to be crucified!" they screamed with voice as one.

When Pilate heard this he was scared and took Christ back inside.
"Where is it that You come from?" asked the Governor, terrified.
But Jesus answered not a word. "Why won't You talk to me?
Don't You realize I have power to destroy or to set free?"

Then Jesus spoke, "Please understand, o'er Me you have no power
Unless it's granted from Above. I came here for this hour!
And so the ones who brought me here retain the greater sin.
You're not really who's in charge. You're only filling in."

Then Pilate tried to set Him free. This trial *he* would end.
The Jews cried, "If you do, we know, you are not Caesar's friend!
For one who claims to be a king must be a rebel, sure!
Rome won't tolerate His release and you'll be out the door!"

When they'd said this, Pilate believed he couldn't do a thing.
And pointing to the Savior said, "I'm giving you your king."
The frenzied mob roared, "Take Him out and have Him crucified!"
"But shall I crucify your king?" the Governor replied.

"We have no king but Caesar!" the chief priests' retorts were loud.
"That's right! No king but Caesar!" came the echo of the crowd.
So Pilate finally gave Him up. So spineless he'd become,
His subjects actually ruled o'er him to see *their* will was done.

Chapter 19:17-27

The soldiers took the Savior then and placed on Him His cross.
They led Him to Golgotha where His garments they did toss
Upon the ground beside Him there. And in between two thieves
They nailed the Lord of Glory to a rough and wooden tree.

Pilate had a sign prepared and placed where all could view.
It read, "Jesus of Nazareth —The King of All the Jews."
Three languages were used to write the message on the board.
The chief priests loudly protested, "That Man is *not* our Lord!"

"You've got to take that placard down," they said with conscience smitten.
Said Pilate, "Absolutely not! I've written what I've written!"
After He'd been lifted up the soldiers took Christ's clothes
And gambled for the choicest one. Who got it? No one knows.

They said, "It is quite precious since it's woven without seam.
And the idea that we'd tear it is a thought we'd never dream."
Thus the Scriptures were fulfilled about the robe that Jesus wore.
"They will cast lots for My clothing," had been scribed long years before.

Now huddled near the cross of Christ four women mourned and wept.
Two of them were relatives - His mother and his aunt.
Another one was Clopas' wife who stood in disbelief
Along side Mary (Magdala) who couldn't hide her grief

When Jesus saw this group below (with one disciple who
Christ never did not stop loving), He decided what He'd do,
And looking towards His mother, He said, "Woman, there's your son."
Then He looked towards that disciple and His eyes said, "He's the one."

That *disciple* understood that Jesus meant for him to care
For His mother, and from that day on his home he gladly shared.

Chapter 19:28-42

Jesus, knowing that His mission was just about complete,
Spoke with labored breathing to those gathered at His feet.
"I am thirsty!" said the Savior. It was just before He died.
He was actually quoting Scripture and those words were prophesied.

Some wine vinegar was handy so they soaked a sponge in it
And they offered it to Jesus on a stick to reach His lips.
Jesus tasted what they'd given, then proclaimed with His last breath,
"IT IS FINISHED!" He declared as He released His Soul in death.

'Twas the day of preparation with the Sabbath coming on,
So the Jews requested Pilate that he'd take the bodies down.
"Please command their legs be broken then their death will faster be.
It would desecrate the Sabbath if we left them on the tree."

So the soldiers came and broke the legs of those on either side.
But when they got to Jesus they saw He'd already died.
Then one of them, who had a spear, thrust it in Jesus' side.
And blood and water poured out from the wound that opened wide.

And he who saw bears witness to the things here written down.
You can believe his word is true —his evidence is sound.
Though Christ did not control it, still the Scriptures were fulfilled,
That "His bones would not be broken," even though He would be killed.

Another thing the Scriptures say, in chapter and in verse,
Is "Someday they will look upon the One whom they have pierced."

Now Joseph of Arimathea, a disciple who'd held back,
Came to Pilate and reported that Christ's death was now a fact.
And he asked to have permission to remove Christ from the cross.
He feared the Jews no longer and could not disguise his loss.

Pilate agreed and so Joseph came, to take Christ's body down.
He was joined by Nicodemus, who brought spice – a hundred pounds.
They wrapped Christ's body with linen, the way Jews bury their dead,
And handled Him so tenderly as they wiped His brow and head.

Close to Calvary was a garden with a tomb where none was laid.
They knew Sabbath was near coming as the light began to fade.
So because they had to hurry and the tomb was close at hand,
The interred the Savior's body, working faster than they'd planned.

Over Sabbath Jesus rested for His work was truly done.
And His Father may have whispered, "Well done good and faithful One!"

Chapter 20:1-18

Early Sunday morning, just before the break of dawn,
Mary Magdalene arrived and found the soldiers were all gone.
She discovered that the stone and seals had all been rolled away
So she ran to Simon Peter and to John, to breathless say,

"They have taken the Lord's body. It's no longer in the tomb.
He is missing. Someone stole Him and the Romans must know whom."
In a flash the two disciples started running for the place,
And the one who wasn't Peter was the winner of that race.

As he stood there breathing deeply, he chose not to go inside,
But peering through the entrance he saw linens lying by.
Just as soon as *he* arrived there, Peter entered, filled with grief,
And he also saw the linens as he stared in disbelief.

For the portion of the wrapping that had been around Christ's head
Wasn't folded with the others but lay neatly by instead.
And Who'd ever done the folding placed it over by itself
In a spot quite easily noticed, near the entrance, on a shelf.

After Peter went inside at last the other did so too.
And what he saw convinced him that the words of Christ were true.
(Though at first they had forgotten what the Scriptures plainly said
Regarding the Messiah who would rise up from the dead.)

The two disciples left then and returned to their own home.
But Mary, who'd come back again, stood weeping all alone.
Through tears she looked inside and saw two white-robed angels there.
She hadn't seen them enter so in wonderment she stared.

One sat just beside the head of where Christ had been put.
The other angel who was there was sitting near the foot.

The angels gently spoke to her and said, "Why do you cry?
You're sobbing uncontrollably. Please tell the reason why?"
So brokenly she told them, "They have taken away my Lord.
And I don't know who took Him or the place where He's been stored."

After she had said these words, she turned and saw Christ there,
Though she didn't recognize Him since her eyes were full of tears.
"Woman, tell me why you're weeping, who're you looking for?" He asked.
But she thought Him just a gardener out to tend his morning tasks.

"Sir," she said, "if You have taken my Lord's body somewhere near,
Please just show me where You've laid Him – I'll take Him away from here.
For my brother's tomb is empty, just outside of Bethany.
I could put Him there and tend Him. Where He is I want to be!"

Then the Savior, with compassion, said her name so tenderly,
That she knew it must be Jesus and she fell down at His feet.

"Oh Rabboni!" she exclaimed with joy and to His ankles held.
"Don't detain Me," He responded. "To My Father I'm compelled
To return. I've not ascended and He's waiting eagerly!
We will soon be reunited! I can hardly wait to see!"

"But I have a message for you, to be given to My men.
Tell them I go to My Father but I'll see them soon again.
And since I was victorious over death and over sin,
He is now *their* Father also, because satan didn't win."

Mary joyfully left that garden, the first herald to proclaim
To the world and His disciples - there is power in His name!

"I have seen Him," she exulted. "I have talked with Him as well.
And He gave to me a message that forever I will tell!
He's our Lord and our Redeemer and the Father loves us too!
It's Good News! It is the Gospel, and I'm telling it to you!"

Chapter 20:19-31

Now later Sunday evening, hiding out because of fear,
The disciples were astonished when the Savior did appear.
He was suddenly among them, though the door they'd locked secure,
And He said, "My peace be with you!" as around Him they drew near.

Then He showed them all the nail scars in His hands and in His side.
And again He told them, "Be at peace! You do not need to hide.
Just as the Father sent Me here, I am sending you now too."
And He breathed on them the Spirit and He gave them work to do.

"You are heralds of forgiveness. You must spread the news afar.
Man's redemption's been accomplished! Heaven's gate is now ajar!"
Thomas, one of the disciples, wasn't there when Jesus came.
So he doubted when the others told him, "He's alive again!"

"There's no way I will believe that!" he retorted with a sneer.
"And no way will you convince me that the Savior has been here!
I will *not* believe your story till I see with my own eyes
And with *them* behold the nail scars and the wound that's in His side."

It was only a week later they were in that house again.
But though the doors were tightly locked, Jesus appeared within.

"Peace to you!" He spoke again, and then to Thomas said,
"I understand you don't believe I've risen from the dead?
So put your finger here and touch the scars in both My hands.
And feel the scar that's on My side, so you can understand."

"Please cease to doubt. You must believe. Don't think this is a fraud."
Then humbly Thomas knelt and said, "You are my Lord and God!"
Jesus responded, "You believe because of what you *see*.
More blessed are the ones who trust though they have not seen Me!"

Jesus did a whole lot more than I've recorded here!
But these things I have written down, so you don't need to fear.
You can believe that Jesus is the Son of God. It's true!
And if you trust in Jesus' name, I promise He'll save you!

Chapter 21:1-25

Later Christ appeared again
While walking on a beach of sand.
Some of His friends, on Galilee,
Had fished all night, but futilely.

The group included James and John
While Peter also came along.
Thomas, the Twin, was there as well
And with him was Nathanael.

Two more rounded out the crew
Who said to Peter, "We'll come too."
They'd fished all night, as I have said,
But caught no fish and had no bread.

At crack of dawn Christ stood ashore
But Who it was they were unsure.
He called out, "Boys, what have you caught?"
They answered Him, "Our work's for naught."

"Cast on the right," He said to them.
"You'll catch so much you'll sink or swim."
They did exactly as He said,
While He stayed on shore, baking bread.

Then John said, "It must be the Lord!"
And Peter, when he'd heard those words,
Stripped off his shirt and dove right in
And eagerly began to swim.

The others stayed on board to haul
And found their net completely full.
When they reached shore the waiting Cook
Checked out their catch and fishes took.

"We'll add these to the ones right here,"
He said, as they were drawing near.
Then Peter helped to drag the net
Which, full of fishes, never split.

"Now come to breakfast," Jesus said,
And served them from His fish and bread.
They knew Him then, but all refrained
To speak out loud His precious name.

This was the third time Christ appeared
To His disciples gathered here,
Since that sad Friday when He'd died
On Calvary's cross - The Crucified.

When they had all eaten their fill
Jesus questioned, "Peter, well?
Do you love Me even more
Than do these gathered on this shore?"

"Yes, Lord," Peter gave reply,
"You know I'll love You till I die."
"Then feed My lambs," Christ said to him,
Before repeating the question.

"Simon, do you love Me true?"
Simon said, "You know I do!"
"Then watch the sheep as well," Christ said.
And then, as though his thoughts He read,

He asked Peter a third time more,
As they were standing on that shore.
"Simon, do you love Me true?"
(The question hurt him through and through.)

He said, "Lord You know everything
About my heart, for You're the King.
I love You and I always will,
Far more than words could ever tell."

Again Christ said, "So feed My sheep,
And then My joy I know you'll keep."

"But one more thing I have to say:
When you were young you went *your* way.
You did what you would choose to do
But when you're old *they'll* carry you."

Christ told him this that he might know
Just how he'd die, when he must go.
"But," Jesus said, "just follow Me.
All will be well eventually."

Then Peter turned and noticed John
Who was behind, tagging along,
And Peter asked, "What about him?
Can You tell me how *he* will end?"

Said Jesus, "That, you cannot know.
His future to you I'll not show.
If he should live till I return
Is not for you to know or learn."

"I only have one job for you -
Just follow Me, I'll see you through."

Some thought they'd actually heard Christ say
One of those men would live always.
But He'd just said, "What's that to you?"
And not that John would live clear through.

That man is me. I wrote this book
From records which I faithfully took.
I promise all I wrote is true
And there are blessings here for you!

He lived with us, Immanuel.
For centuries now we've tried to tell
About His life on earth with men,
And how one day He'll come *again*.

We've told the stories o'er and o'er
And still we try to tell them more,
Because somehow they don't grow old -
These greatest stories ever told.

If all He did were written down,
A book to hold could not be found.
For all the world could not contain
The stories told about that Name!

Still, we will write and speak and sing
About the Lamb - our *coming* King.
And someday near a sea like fire,
With angels we will sing still higher.

"Worthy, worthy," we will say,
"Is He who stooped to come our way."
And at His feet will be cast down,
By those redeemed, unnumbered crowns.

He Is Risen

For the portion of the wrapping that had been around Christ's head
Wasn't folded with the others but lay neatly by instead.
And Who'd ever done the folding placed it over by itself
In a spot quite easily noticed, near the entrance, on a shelf.
John 20:7